JUST ADD WATER

JUST ADD WATER

A Memoir

JesuMarie

JUST ADD WATER
A MEMOIR

Copyright © 2015 JesuMarie.

iUniverse books may be ordered through booksellers or by contacting:

iUniverse
1663 Liberty Drive
Bloomington, IN 47403
www.iuniverse.com
1-800-Authors (1-800-288-4677)

Because of the dynamic nature of the Internet, any web addresses or links contained in this book may have changed since publication and may no longer be valid. The views expressed in this work are solely those of the author and do not necessarily reflect the views of the publisher, and the publisher hereby disclaims any responsibility for them.

Any people depicted in stock imagery provided by Thinkstock are models, and such images are being used for illustrative purposes only.
Certain stock imagery © Thinkstock.

ISBN: 978-1-4917-7503-5 (sc)
ISBN: 978-1-4917-7502-8 (e)

Library of Congress Control Number: 2015916540

Print information available on the last page.

iUniverse rev. date: 11/10/2015

Contents

Introduction

JesuMarie, who was born and raised in Philadelphia, Pennsylvania, attributes her love of reading to her now-deceased grandmother, an Italian immigrant who could not read or write. She also attributes her educational drive to her Italian father, who made it known to her from a very young age that women are for reproducing, and to whom she was determined to prove that women are capable of so much more than just childbearing.

This book is her attempt to be at peace that she not only made it through all the childhood confusion of domestic abuse and was capable of compiling her own memoir from the child's point of view but that, in addition, she is a resilient individual. She studied resilience as one concept in her doctorate of philosophy education.

Individuals who have experienced domestic abuse will find this book interesting, as it is written from the child's point of view. Women who have been targets of domestic abuse will empathize with the woman who is battered in this book. Perhaps men who have been past abusers will understand their roles in the formation of the psyches of their children who are spectators of that abuse.

JesuMarie is a self-employed author and an adjunct professor of nursing at several universities in the TriCounty area, including Philadelphia.

The new mother handed her brand-new baby girl to her own mother when she arrived home from the hospital. The baby's grandmother had a back deformity from birth, and it took a few moments for her to position the baby safely in her arms. She repeatedly squeezed and kissed the new baby girl, her first grandchild. The baby, fair of face, had hair and eyes as dark as coal. Her lips were as red as the reddest apple. The grandmother felt the baby's specialness and her warmth, and she felt perplexed by the baby's all-knowing eyes, thinking Che regalo (What a gift)! The baby looked this way and that way and didn't miss a beat of the goings-on around her. She was a gift.

The new baby girl felt loved.

1

Chicken

Three times she told me, "Just drown it!" Was she crazy? I could not be a peep killer. It was the day before Easter Sunday. The priest was coming to bless the house. Jesus would be risen tomorrow. I saw the movie; Moses was holding two tablets. This was after the part where he parted the water. The tablet on the right had commandments 1–3. The one on the left had 4–10. And number 5, I knew from Catholic school, was "Thou Shalt Not Kill."

I could go to hell over this one! I was only ten. I didn't have a lot of years left to try to be perfect. I needed time. Three times I put its tiny, yellow, fuzzy head under the spigot. It squirmed, choked, and wiggled like crazy. Three times I pulled it back out of the watery downpour. I thought of Saint Peter. Didn't the nuns teach us that he said he was not Jesus's friend three times? I was definitely not this peep's friend. Then I had a watershed of my own. I could not do it. Whether this peep had a crooked leg or not, I could not commit peep murder.

Just like the time she told me to bring my pet duck Jaffe to my grandmother's house, which was up the street. We lived in a "Father, Son, and Holy Ghost" house across the street from the cemetery. My ducks, Sammy and Jaffe, and my roosters and chickens (they were no-name roosters and chickens; I could not tell them apart) lived in our city yard. The neighbors complained when the roosters crowed in the middle of the night. *Who cares?* I loved the show *Ben Casey* and named my ducks Sam and Jaffe after my favorite actor in the show. I identified with this guy because in the movie *Gunga Din*, he was a second-class citizen too (just like a girl in an Italian family). I got his number—he was a poor water bearer who wanted to be something more. I looked around this neighborhood, spied everybody coming and going, men showing off, women and girls being treated like slaves, and I wanted something more too.

> *Though I've belted you and flayed you,*
> *By the livin' Gawd that made you,*
> *You're a better man than I am, Gunga Din.*

(Kipling, "Gunga Din," stanza 5)

So I walked Jaffe to Grandmom up the Street, and she barely said hello when she grabbed Jaffe out of my folded arms and shut the door, leaving me on the front stoop, thinking, *God, she's in a mood today.* Then I started thinking about poor Sammy. I had come home from grade school, a short two-block walk, and found him walking totally sideways and crooked in the yard. And he kept falling down. *Give me a break!* His webbed feet flapped above his head; he couldn't get up. I ran into the house and confronted the Woman Who Ordered the Peep Assassination.

"Mommy, Mommy! Sammy is a mess! Did you do something to him?"

"Relax," she said. "All I did was wash his dirty feathers with Grandmom up the Street's soap. Now he is clean."

Was she kidding me? The lye soap that Grandmom up the Street made?

"Are you nuts?" I screeched.

Okay, Catholic boys and girls didn't get much of a science education, but any non compos mentis knew you didn't wash a duck with lye soap. How would Sammy live without Jaffe? How could Jaffe live without Sammy? I knew it was written all over my face. I was a nutcase.

I knocked and knocked at Grandmom up the Street's front door, and she did not answer. I went around the alleyway, and her back gate was locked. I went home and told my mother, and she told me to have a cup of coffee. So I waited awhile, read a chapter of *The Diary of Anne Frank*, and had a cup of coffee. The Germans were in the house and searching for Anne's family again. They had not found them yet. I wondered if I would ever see my Jaffe again. Next time I tried, the front door was open, and I just walked in.

"Grandmom?" I was ready to ask, "Where's Jaffe?" but she did not give me a chance. The words from the beginning of *Ben Casey* were screaming in my brain and drowning out what she was saying: "Man, Woman, Birth, Death, Infinity."

She was telling me to sit down. She was putting a Flintstones jelly jar glass of ice water down in front of me. Why was she being so nice all of a sudden? Then I noticed a bowl with a fork beside it on the table too. Then I saw feathers in her sink.

"Eat, Giuditta. You wanna some duck?"

All the adults stuck together. An adult was doing something not right, and I was powerless to do anything about it. I was as good as gold; why were they torturing me like this? I went running from her house to the cemetery across the street. I could not go home and complain; the Woman Who Ordered the Peep Assassination had sent me there with Jaffe in the first place.

I wanted to die, cry out loud, kill myself, and die. I squeezed in between two bent bars of the cemetery's fence and ripped my dress. As I looked up the path in the cemetery, I saw all the familiar tombstones with all the familiar Italian names on them on either side of the cobblestone path. I looked at the cobblestones and swore I saw a lake of water moving toward me. It started near the tall Rossini angel tombstone and flowed toward me. I looked this deal up in my encyclopedia; the moisture and heat were combining, coming up from the ground and producing a mirage, which looked like a waterway. I wanted to drown myself in it. But God did not like suicide, either. No such luck.

He was in the cemetery when I got there. I think he was probably around five years older than I was. He was the son of one of my mother's friends who cooked at the hospital. I had seen her on duty once when I went on a field trip. She wanted me to be a candy striper at the hospital. I wanted to be a nun. So it was interesting that here, before me, was her teenage son, telling me that he wanted to have a baby with me. This guy was looney tunes. I reminded him that I was ten years old. He really did not care. *In the mouth of the wolf* I could get out of here.

"Just lie on top of me and pee," he said.

"Pee?" I said. "What if I don't have to pee right now?"

"Just relax," he said, "and I will pee."

So I ran again. This time, I ran toward the back of the cemetery where the mausoleums were near the other Catholic church, the one where all the Irish people went. Then I noticed the door to my favorite mausoleum was open, so I rushed in. I closed the door and tried to lock myself in. I was trying to hide from Pee Man, but the door would not lock from the inside, so then I ran out of the cemetery and over toward the community pool. I looked through the chain-link fence and saw all the neighborhood kids who could afford it swimming in the pool. I did not have the water privilege then.

So I went over to the Irish church and went in to make my confession. When our sins were really bad, we just switched churches. The priests in this church did not know me; we were three parishes in the same neighborhood. The priests could never keep any of us straight. The nuns knew every hair on our nappy, Italian heads.

"Forgive me, Father, for I have sinned. It has been one-half week since my last confession."

I told Father (who I could not see behind the slide door) that I wanted badly to kill myself because I had tried to drown my peep, I wanted to seriously do a number on the Woman Who Ordered the Peep Assassination for soaping my duck, and I wanted to bury Grandmom up the Street with the fishes for cooking Jaffe. He told me that I needed to forgive others so that Jesus would forgive me.

It made sense. I needed Jesus's forgiveness, and I needed to forgive others.

I was such a guilty mess. I did not have the nerve to tell him about the peeing-in-the-cemetery deal. Mother of God, how many commandments could a kid break in one day? My penance was to say the rosary that night before I went to bed. Great, I did not want to be a nitpicker here, but now I had one more thing I had to do.

No problem. My rosary was hanging on my headboard at home. Three Dracula movies in a row at the movie theater. After the movies, we had the *hearts of rabbits*. We came home scared to death and put our light-up-in-the-dark rosary beads around our necks and went to sleep. Dracula was afraid of Jesus on the cross. Who wouldn't be? The guy looked scary.

I remembered seeing a movie where penitentiary women were being hosed down with a water cannon for punishment. They could not stay standing. The force of the water kept knocking them down. Did my Sammy feel like that when he fell? He just could not get up again. And then he stayed down forever. I stayed with him and baptized him in the name of the Father and the Son and the Holy Ghost just in case his mother did not have a chance or was not a Catholic. I did not pour water on his head. I figured he had enough water during his lye bath by the Woman Who Ordered the Peep Assassination, and I let that part go.

From what I could tell, water bugs (the big black, shiny ones) never had a problem like the penitentiary women or my Sammy. They came out to play when water was everywhere. If you did not watch where you were walking at night, you might get a nice, big, wet, squishy surprise. They crawled up the strap of your flip-flop, onto your foot, and over to the other side. The time the water heater burst, they were everywhere—floating in the water in the basement, crawling up the concrete walls, climbing on top of the coal in the bin, going up the stairs and then into the kitchen sideways through the doorjamb. I wished that I could go sideways to somewhere and disappear.

I said my aspirations, "Oh, Sacred Heart of Jesus, I place my trust in Thee." That's what they taught us.

Say them.

Say them again.

Say them over and over again, fifty million times, when we needed help. I went home, picked up #1 Italian Son and the Midigan (more on this later) and we walked to the Moses fountain in the park. We climbed into the fountain under the statue and didn't even take our sneakers off. As we sat in the fountain together, I looked up at Moses standing there with the commandment tablets in one hand and the other hand raised up. Was he praying? Was he trying to scratch a mosquito on his nose? Funny, he did not look like Charlton Heston, and he did not ask you to put a bathing suit on. I had bonded with Moses. He was a sinner too; he probably knew how hard I always tried. This guy was not a chicken; he knew how to play it. He parted that water and took his people with him through the middle of the Red Sea. I hoped Jesus forgave him. I hoped I was forgiven too, forgiven of attempted peep murder. I was trying to forgive the Woman Who Ordered the Peep Assassination and Grandmom up the Street so that Jesus would forgive me.

I thought of drowning myself in the foot and a half of water in the fountain, but the thing was that I had #1 Italian Son and the Midigan to take care of here. If I drowned myself, how would they get home? Wasn't it already bad enough that I crossed the street that we were not allowed to cross to get here? Favorite Cousin tried to hit us up so she could come with us where Moses lived with his tablets in the fountain. I told her no, I had enough to take care of with #1 Italian Son and the Midigan. As soon as she could not see us anymore (we were fountain bound), she went home and told the Italian Madman that we had crossed the street.

The nun in school used to always say that a human being could live for a month without food but only about a week without water. She even said that most of our bodies were water. Sorry, Sister, I could not believe that one. My body did not look like water. It didn't even feel like water. I was busy trying to float in the foot and a half of water, trying to squeeze in a few more aspirations, and trying to figure out what Moses meant with that finger up (not the middle one—I could have figured that one out) when #1 Italian Son started splashing like crazy and jumping up and down in the water.

He saw the Italian Madman coming before I did. The floodgates were open. I knew I was the one who had to suffer. I was the oldest, and I was a girl.

I remembered the Woman Who Ordered the Peep Assassination telling me that when I was born in the hospital, the Italian Madman came to visit, and when he found out that I was a girl, the guards had to remove him for acting "crazy." I always wondered what acting "crazy" meant. I always knew it wasn't good. My relationship with him was shot to pieces from the very beginning.

The Italian Madman pulled me home by my hair; in the living room, I was trying to do a breast stroke through a sea of whips with his belt. The worst part was the Woman Who Ordered the Peep Assassination sitting in the kitchen having coffee with Lizzy the Store while I received my just due. There was no escape. No, the worst was trying to run up the stairs and him grabbing me back and making me sit on my backside where the belt had done its dirty work. The gig was up. Where was my guardian angel when I needed her? When I tried to soak in a cold tub of water, #1 Italian Son kept coming in the bathroom. No locks on the bathroom door in those days. We had five people in the house most of the time—the Italian Madman, the Woman Who Ordered the Peep Assassination, #1 Favorite Son, Midigan, and me.

One bathroom and no privacy in this house.

Then the mother took the new baby girl home to the father and to a house where the father beat the mother. The father did not look in the direction of the baby girl. The baby girl could not comprehend her pain but internalized it nonetheless.

The baby girl felt afraid.

2

Garlic

The Italian Madman lined up all the garlic in the tomato salad on his knife and then slipped the whole amount into his mouth. A whole bottle of Listerine would not do the trick on his breath. The food had to be totally cooked, cooled, and ready for him to eat when he walked in the front door after work.

Once, the transit bus was running late. The food order had just arrived from the Italian food market, and I had lined up the milk, pumpkin pie (it was around Thanksgiving), half gallon of ice cream, and all the food at one end of the table. The chicken was cooking in the oven at 350 degrees. It was hard for my twelve-year-old self to be a student and the chief cook and bottle washer; I was *cooked like a lobster* myself.

So my timing was a little off. The Italian Madman finished his salad, and the chicken was not done cooking, so he turned the whole kitchen table over, and everything got broken and squished. The half-gallon glass bottle broke, squished the pie, and mixed with the broken jar of applesauce. It all went down. American bread, Italian rolls, cotechino, cappicola, and genoa salami all flattened by the weight of the table with the blue teapot design.

Around that time, the Woman Who Ordered the Peep Assassination walked in the kitchen from work. The Italian Madman picked up the long fork from the stove and tried to stab her in the face with it. She moved just as the fork went deep into the woodwork around the kitchen door.

That did it for me.

I ran as fast as I could to the farthest place I could reach in a hurry—to Grandmom up the Street. Meanwhile, the Italian Madman pulled the roasting pan with the chicken out of the oven and dumped it on the Woman Who Ordered the Peep Assassination. She was screaming (I could hear her up the street), "Thank You, God, I am not burned! I am not burned!"

It all felt like a real-life *Twilight Zone*.

A small miracle, she said later. What's up, Doc, with that? When the leper asked Jesus, "Lord, if You are willing, You can make me clean," I do not think the leper had a small miracle on his diseased mind. Sister said there are no small miracles. That's right, Sister. When Jesus said, "Be clean," the leper was cured. But the hitch was Jesus told the leper he could not tell anyone. Kinda like me; I could never tell anybody this stuff. They would never believe me.

Grandmom up the Street saw me coming from the front window where she used to sit and crochet. Then she asked me (like she always did), "Mah, Giuditta, whatsa *matta* fah you?"

How could I keep this a secret? The Italian Madman was trying to kill the Woman Who Ordered the Peep Assassination, and I was a key witness.

"Grandmom! He is after me."

So she shoved me behind the front door and then went to close the door, only she never made it, because he was there on her stoop, and he pushed her against the wall and pushed his way into the house. He was looking for me and went past her into the house. Meanwhile, I was behind the door and scared to death. The only problem was that he saw me on his way back out of the house and then pulled me home by my hair.

"Clean it up, *la strega*!" he hollered.

I could not figure this one out. He was the one who made the mess, and I had to clean it up? And he was calling me a witch in Italian! The Italian Madman was a bricklayer who possessed a lot of physical power. The old Italian ladies on the street called him "house devil, street angel." The old Italian men told a story of when he was riding a horse in the neighborhood when he was a young man. The horse would not obey, so what did he do? He got off the horse and punched it in the face. They all said he could really *sweat seven shirts* as a bricklayer.

On a normal night, after he ate a dinner that was cooked, perfectly prepared, and cooled, he would take a nap.

"Call me at seven o'clock," he would command.

What if I didn't want to? What if I was busy? What if I wanted to take a nap myself? Did he think he was the only tired one around here? He would get up after his nap, shower, put on Old Spice, and take off to take care of his garlic breath with a few highballs at the Italian club around the corner. I always wondered how many highballs he had before he came home, half-lit, around nine o'clock at night to beat the Woman Who Ordered the Peep Assassination for simple stuff—the garlic in the tomato salad was not cut up small enough, he did not like her attitude. Maybe he would be a different person, maybe he would be kind, if he went on the water wagon.

One time when he came home, he loaded his gun and pushed it into her hands, daring her to shoot him. When she pulled the trigger and it misfired, he beat her because she pulled the trigger. When she talked, he did not like it. When she was quiet, he did not like it. He did not like #1 Italian Son, either, and he totally ignored the Midigan and me. When he found #1 Italian Son's hiding place for his cigarettes (under the heating vent in *my* bedroom on the third floor), he went ape-o. He pulled the whole shipping trunk (a Paulie the Junkman special for fifty cents) full of Atlas comic books down to the pavement (around three hundred of them) and left the trunk at the curb for the trashman to pick up. The Italian Madman had better confess this one! Only he never went to church or confession. I hoped that Jesus would not forgive him for this one. How could I forgive him? Add another sin to the list for my Saturday confession trip.

When the Italian Madman was finished beating #1 Italian Son, the kitchen looked like a bomb hit it. Cabinets were turned over, food from the icebox was all over the floor, and the icebox had dents in it. #1 Italian Son had a bloody nose and a black eye, and I was headed to the convent around the corner. Where were the Fantastic Four when a girl needed them? Out on the pavement, inside a shipping trunk, waiting for the trashman to come and get them.

"He's still your father," the Woman Who Ordered the Peep Assassination would tell us fifty million times a day.

I caught myself wondering all the time how the Midigan felt. We weren't even his family, and he was stuck with us. At least he wasn't another big mahoff like some of the Italian men around here. He had been with us since he was two years old, dropped off by his mother, who had to work and could not care for him and ended up never coming back to get him. I would try to see what she looked like each time she dropped fifteen dollars in an envelope off for a week's babysitting inside the front-door mail slot. One time, I did see her. She reminded me of Susan Hayward in *Back Street*.

I found out by listening to Grandmom down the Alley talk in Italian that the Midigan's real mother was a waitress, and her boyfriend made a man kneel down in the restaurant where she worked, and then he shot him in the head close up for flirting with her. The poor guy's hands and feet were tied up, and he was in a kneeling position, execution-style—this was a special way of dying for a special person. Who died and left that murderer boss? Perry Mason could do a real-life number on the murderer and convince him to admit his guilt.

The Midigan looked like a peaceful kind of guy on the surface, but he was always doing something he should not be doing with #1 Italian Son. The old Italian ladies said he was born with a chip on his shoulder. #1 Italian Son and the Midigan: a regular

Batman-and-Robin duo. The picture changed when Favorite Cousin joined forces with them—then they became Larry, Moe, and Curly.

One day, when the Three Stooges were outside playing and I was on my way up to the third floor (I had this habit of counting the steps as I went up—they stayed the same; they never changed), I heard this gurgling kind of water sound coming from the bathroom. I looked in to see the Italian Madman strangling the Woman Who Ordered the Peep Assassination while she was sitting on the toilet. She must have been leaning on the flusher, because I could hear the toilet flushing again and again, underneath the gurgling sounds she was making as he was choking her. Big-time water waste here. If I did not get involved, I knew I would have to go to purgatory to atone. And the faucet was running in the tub too. Was he strangling her first and then getting ready to make it look like she drowned in the tub? The Woman Who Ordered the Peep Assassination's arms and legs were jerking up and down. The Italian Madman had probably hit a nerve. Was this her Waterloo? I could not hang her out to dry. The water clock was ticking.

I ran up to the third floor, looked out the window, and saw my old Italian man neighbor sitting on the front stoop. I called out to him in my loudest voice. My mind was racing, my vision was blocked, my heart was trying to escape out of my chest, and I could not breathe; I was stuck in one spot.

"Help! My father is choking my mother! Help! Call the police!" I screamed out the window in my loudest voice.

Only I could not hear me. Turns out, my mind was playing tricks on me; I only *thought* I called out. My mind heard my voice scream the words, but the words were stuck in my throat and could not make it over my tongue and out of my mouth. I knew the police would come if somebody could call them. They knew us. They were at my house all the time. I was scared to death again.

Once when I was learning how to drive and my cousin was taking me for a test drive in the Italian Madman's Bonneville, we got lost. The feeling when we were lost was the same feeling I was having now on the third floor of my house. I was rooted in one spot like the Spirit of God tree on my block (the only one for blocks—that's my name for her). I could not think, I could not see, my heart was having a thunderstorm, and worst of all, I could not *breathe*. The Italian Madman was strangling my mother, and then he was going to drown her. I felt like I was strangling with her. I could not wear turtlenecks after this episode.

She did not have much to work with, but the Woman Who Ordered the Peep Assassination really always tried to be a good mother to us and a good wife to the Italian Madman. She was the oldest of four siblings. All the adjustments Grandmom down the Alley needed to make when she came from Italy in 1929 rested on her shoulders, and she had to learn English in order to go to school. When she came home speaking English, her father asked her what language she was speaking, and when she said, "Americano," he slapped her across her face.

"Noan you forgetta, you Italiana."

The way she told it, her three younger sisters were wilder than she was. She was the dreaded oldest. Grandmom down the Alley beat her with her hands, a broom, the Bible, a pot, a spatula—whatever she could get her hands on. The worst part was that the Woman Who Ordered the Peep Assassination did not trust Grandmom down the Alley for a split second. Now that I think about it, that is how I feel about the Woman Who Ordered the Peep Assassination now.

She used to tell me she never ate a hot dog or American food. It never occurred to her to ask why her mother (Grandmom down the Alley) called a loaf of white bread "American bread." Her father died from a stab wound that he had gotten in the Italian bar up the street. The last time she saw him, the ambulance men were putting him on a stretcher, and when she ran up to kiss him, an old Italian lady pulled her back. When the Woman Who Ordered the Peep Assassination was seven years old, Grandmom down the Alley married Poppy (the Tastykake/Medicine Man—more on him later).

Life was not happy for her. When she was a teenager, she ate to make herself happy. Every day after school, she stopped by the corner pharmacy, which had a soda fountain, and bought a banana split. She sat there and ate it and then went home and gave Grandmom down the Alley all her pay. She barely graduated high school and did not like to read. She loved doing things with her hands. She worked in a millinery shop, where she could sew to her heart's content. I like to look at a certain picture of her in the only family album we have. At the bottom of the picture, someone had written "1950"—the year I was born. She looks very thin. She told me once that it was taken right before she found out she was pregnant with me and right after the Italian Madman had hit her for the first time and punched her in the stomach.

I read in order to fall asleep if saying the rosary didn't work. And I always use the Joyful Mysteries, kind of like wishful thinking on my part. I wanted my life to be joyful, like part of Jesus's life was joyful.

It was a dark, cold, middle-of-the-winter night. I had fallen asleep reading Daphne Du Maurier's *Rebecca*. The roosters and chickens were quiet in the yard for a change. The house was quiet except for the faucet dripping in the bathroom and this thud sound that I keep hearing over and over again. I counted twenty-three thuds before I got up to investigate. Sherlock Holmes would have been proud of me. Sometimes I wished I had a Watson to help me out here.

I crept around the hallway on the second floor when I realized the thud sound was coming from the Woman Who Ordered the Peep Assassination and the Italian Madman's bedroom. I secretly approached the doorway, but the thuds had stopped. He was frozen in space and time on top of her; he heard me coming before I knew that he was the thud maker. She was bleeding from her eyes, nose, mouth. When I told him to stop, he told me to make like Casper the Friendly Ghost and disappear, or the same thing would happen to me.

Funny thing. All Casper wanted was a friend. Like I did. Who would be my friend with this crazy family? *Why*, I wondered, *do so many scary things begin with a* G? Gallows, gangrene, German measles, ghoul, glacier, goblin, grave. Not like homonyms that sounded alike but had different meanings, such as bear and bear; not like synonyms that sounded different but had the same meanings such as fly, flit, hover, wing, glide, soar, dart; not antonyms that had opposite meanings, such as excited or calm. Maybe I could call these scary *G* words "scaryms."

The one tree on my city street was right in front of my house. I learned in science class that a tree can be 75 percent water. The way I figured it, it could still be hard enough to do the trick. I prayed a part of the Our Father:

Our Father, who art in heaven, hallowed be Thy name.

Then I added:

Please let the Spirit of God tree fall on him, knock him off my mother, and squash him.

Squash his black spirit just like a black water bug. I waited. It did not happen. So I ran downstairs and dialed the number for the police. He was on me, pulling me away from the phone. The Woman Who Ordered the Peep Assassination and I were outside the front door in a flash. She was in her bra and slip.

Her face was bloody.

I was *matta*.

This guy had guts. He taunted the policemen outside from the top step of the stoop. He only had boxer shorts on.

"I know the law, you motherf———ers. Six inches from my front door is my property, and you can't touch me."

This guy coulda been somebody. Like Marlon Brando in the movie *On the Waterfront*, he could have been a contender. So one policeman grabbed him by the ankle and pulled him down the three front steps. It took four policemen to throw him in the red paddy wagon. I counted one policeman for each arm and each leg. Of course, #1 Italian Son and the Midigan were still asleep. I was cheering the policemen on. And what did the Woman Who

Ordered the Peep Assassination do? She pushed me away from her and ordered, "Watch your mouth, and go upstairs and get his pants."

Watch my mouth? I wanted to ask her how a person could watch her mouth when her eyes were stuck on her face above her mouth. Did I need to use a mirror to watch my mouth? That could be a problem, since I didn't happen to have a mirror with me there in the middle of the night, tucked in my underwear.

Get his pants? I wanted to scream. *Get his pants?* He just beat you up. You are a bloody mess, I am outside in my panties here on the friggin' sidewalk (I mentally recorded this curse sin for Saturday at the other church), and you want me to *get his pants?* Love is a powerful thing. So is hate. Love and hate mixed together are lethal, crazy-making emotions. How could I ever play out on the street again after this episode?

And so, when they kept him in jail for a while to calm down, it was a wonderful, peaceful time at home. When he came home, it started again. When he acted up, the four of us carried our mattresses on our heads to Grandmom up the Alley's two-bedroom house, where she lived with Poppy and Favorite Cousin. So there they were, the three of them in a two-bedroom house, and here we come, the four of us, down the alley. Seven people, two bedrooms—you do the math; we were an improper-fraction family.

"Mah, I tella them all the time. Noan you fight. Noboby a listena to me," Poppy kept saying.

We were all adrift on the Atlantic Ocean, survivors of the *Titanic*, trying to outswim the Italian Madman. It seemed like we were always leaving the house and going to live with my grandmother down the alley for a temporary stay. Grandmom down the Alley never refused us. She just made more tomato salad with garlic and fried peppers. Poppy just kept telling us, "Noan you fight."

Grandmom down the Alley would take a stand right away when she saw us coming down the alley.

"Mah, that somna bitch."

Funny, did she realize she was cursing out the Italian Madman's mother (Grandmom up the Street) and not him when she said that? Grandmom down the Alley could say *bitch* in English; I knew she would confess it too. We were not allowed to curse. If you said it, even if you thought it, you had to confess it. The colored girls on Grandmom down the Alley's street told me that *bitch* means "being in total control of herself." Amen, my sister. I could get with that in no time.

The Italian Madman always tried to reclaim us. When he did, Grandmom down the Alley always shut the door in his face. The Italian Madman did not fight her the way he fought his own mother. I couldn't figure that one out. She had a big hump on her back like the humpback whale I saw on *The Undersea World of Jacques Cousteau* once. Humpback whales are usually found near the coast, looking for food, and they have long flippers. Grandmom down the Alley was always found near my house looking for the oceanic whitetip shark hunting its prey, which happened to be my mother. I imagined Grandmom down the Alley smacking the Italian Madman with her huge flippers and knocking him for a loop into the Pacific Ocean far away.

We were learning picture study in school. Why did we have to look at plain old pictures that didn't make sense? Why were we wasting time like this? Didn't Sister say we would spend time in purgatory for wasted paper and wasted *time*? Who cares that the rich French people were upset about Millet's *The Gleaners*? It was just a picture of three poor people picking wheat. Some rich people need to give it up. We could have been reading a book.

I thought of a picture now that I discovered on my own when I was reading the *Encyclopedia Britannica* from cover to cover—yep, A–Z, over the summer. It was called *Watson and the Shark*. I gave the picture my own meaning, like Sister said you should do. Grandmom down the Alley was a man with long black hair trying to stab a huge shark in the water. Of course, the Italian Madman was the shark in the water who was trying to kill the Woman Who Ordered the Peep Assassination (who was a naked man in the water, some of it pink). In the boat with Grandmom down the Alley were three men (I pretended they were #1 Italian Son, Favorite Cousin, and the Midigan) looking sad. The guy behind Grandmom down the Alley was Poppy letting her do her thing and saying, "Noan you fight."

Then there was a man who was directing two other guys who were trying to pull the Woman Who Ordered the Peep Assassination in from the water before the shark could get her. I made this guy Fat Federico from the neighborhood, who was a mongoloid and very strong. I never could understand how he could be a mongoloid and be Italian too. When I had time, I needed to look that up.

The two guys hanging off the boat and trying to reach the Woman Who Ordered the Peep Assassination and pull her into the boat were me and my guardian angel, Desiree. I had named my guardian angel Desiree after I read a historical novel about Napoleon's exile on the island of Elba and a woman he loved there by the name of Desiree. Napoleon could have been one of us. His picture in the *Encyclopedia Britannica* shows him as short with dark hair. He loved the Italians on that island, and they loved him. He even made a bunch of changes that he is remembered for there, like cleaning up the stray dog population.

We needed Napoleon here in the neighborhood; there were always dogs with foamy mouths roaming around. The last guy in the picture I envisioned as Charles up the Street. He was the only colored man on the boat; he lived next door to Grandmom Up the Street and had stolen #1 Italian Son's watch. That was when #1 Italian Son was still small and could not pick up for himself. So I did. I knocked on Charles up the Street's door, grabbed him by his shirt, and made him pay up. He gave me a Barney Rubble jelly jar with the watch inside it. I was glad not just because I got the watch back but because I did not have Barney Rubble yet in my collection. I thought this watch episode merited Charles up the Street being a part of the picture; he had paid his dues.

It was great being at Grandmom down the Alley's house. We never had to choke on our food. There was no shed that housed dogs that were connected somehow and never any pink or green Irish food on the floor (more on this another time). Things were calm and not crazy. We could sleep at night. Crowded up, like fifty million minnows in a small pond, the four of us slept in a little living room with our mattresses on the floor, but we were happy. Bedtime was bedtime, not let-the-show-begin time.

We didn't miss school, and we certainly didn't miss the Water Ice Man. He came on Grandmom down the Alley's street even before our street. He had his four-wheeled little cart, he shaved the big block of ice in front of us, and then he let us pick the flavor we wanted. He even sold pretzels that were on the bottom tray right above the wheels. This old, chubby guy could move along. He was so patient with us. Small, chubby, kind, Italian speaking, and nice to kids. We needed all the niceness we could get. Life in this neighborhood could be rough.

Grandmom down the Alley told me when she was born, her farmer parents went into town and borrowed a rug from a rich man. They put her in the rug and rolled it up as tightly as they could. Then each one of them took an end of the rug and wrung it very hard (kind of like a human saltwater taffy from Wildwood) to try to straighten out her back. It didn't work.

We had just returned home from Grandmom's down the Alley when it was the night of the eighth-grade graduation dance. Things had simmered down, probably because of the fifty million aspirations I said every day.

Save Your servant who hopes in You, O my God.

I was upstairs getting dressed when the Italian Madman and the Woman Who Ordered the Peep Assassination were at it again. He was throwing 45 rpm records across the dining-room table at her (good-bye to "Kansas City" for good), and she was throwing dishes (that she got free at the movie theater) at him. So I sneaked past the two of them and called my date on the phone. One phone in the house and it had a party line. I could not hear anyone speaking on the phone. I was in the clear.

I was outside by the curb on the cobblestone street watching the trolleys go by in my fancy dress and dyed pumps. I apologized to my date, no pictures here tonight, palsy-walsy.

"No problem," he said. "Everyone in the neighborhood is afraid of your father. I wouldn't go in there if you paid me a million bucks."

When the baby girl turned two years old, the mother brought a new baby home from the hospital. A baby boy. The father was so excited. The grandmother tried to squeeze and kiss the new baby boy, her first grandson. The baby, fitful and full of fire, did not want to be squeezed and kissed. The grandmother thought, He is just like his father, the man who beats my daughter.

The toddler girl felt abandoned.

3

Bay Leaf

I remember looking down the stairs when I heard the fire engine late one night. It sounded like the fire engine was in the house. The Italian Madman was on the floor playing with #1 Italian Son and a shiny fire engine truck. The Woman Who Ordered the Peep Assassination sat on the gray living room chair and watched the whole thing. She was an accomplice. What a beautiful family scene! Only I wasn't there. The Midigan wasn't, either. We were not invited. I was a second-class citizen with no chance for advancement, ever—a goldfish they would keep in a fishbowl and feed every day.

Food was everywhere. It was part of my Italian culture. When they sold Mallo Cups at grade school recess, I thought I died and went to heaven. We never had candy in the house. But then, who could even afford candy at recess? Mallo Cups looked like a small cup. I saved the play-money cardboard inserts that came with them. They were good for future cashing in. If you could not afford a Mallo Cup on your kid budget, you could always buy the two-cent Chunky bar.

So it made sense that the Woman Who Ordered the Peep Assassination would try to use food to free her (and us)—like the time she put rat poison in his macaroni and meatballs. Rats were smart enough to wait awhile after they ate something to see if they got sick. If they did not, they would eat more. For sure, there are no Italian rats then. Because an Italian rat would *mangia* like there was no tomorrow, not wait, and keep stuffing his face until he died.

Rat poison placed several good things in our corner of the ring. It was odorless and colorless. So she called me, and we were both watching him stuff his face with the spaghetti and meatballs. We waited together for the *death of the pope*.

Then I felt something scratchy on the back of my neck. I thought it was my guilty conscience when I turned to see that I was leaning up against all the poked holes in the woodwork from the time he tried to stab her in the face with the chicken fork. Now I felt vindicated. I looked this word up in Paulie the Junkman's dictionary (more on my favorite book later); it means "set free, delivered." Yep, we all needed to be set free and delivered from the Italian Madman.

The ending would be quick; we knew it. He would fall dead to the kitchen floor, I would call the police (remember, I knew the number by heart), and he would be gone from this earth forever. I knew he had mortal sins on his soul, and he never went to confession. The devil would welcome him; they knew each other from way back.

The chicken was prepared and cooled, the garlic was minced just right, and he was lining up the garlic from the salad on his knife like he always did. This time, though, he would never make it to the Listerine bottle in the bathroom. He would only be a memory at the Italian club. We watched and waited together for him to choke and die. But he didn't. He did not even flinch. There was no way out for the Woman Who Ordered the Peep Assassination, #1 Italian Son, the Midigan, or me.

I dreamed of a time when I would see his name engraved on a tombstone in the cemetery, and he would be gone. I willed the rain to come down; a huge monsoon moving in from Atlantic City would wash him away, cars out front would be floating, the tree out front would be uprooted. The deal would be cinched.

But he just kept eating. Rat poison could not even kill him. He had absorbed the spirit of Psycho-Man when he threw away our comic books. A tidal wave could not get rid of him. He was too strong. I wanted him to sink in quicksand like Cheyenne and that Indian chief.

Only I did not want him to come out.

The Italian Madman got really mad when the dog up the alley kept barking, especially when he was trying to take his after-work nap. The dog barked every time somebody walked up or down the alley.

Which was all the time.

Kids were always cutting up and down the alley and taking the shortcut between two streets. Even adults took shortcuts up and down the alley. Rosie the Store was up the alley, and people went there to get eggs, milk, bread, and candy. The dog was fenced in but jumped at you when you walked by.

I was mopping the kitchen floor with Spic and Span after dinner and on my five hundredth repeat of *Jesus, meek and humble of heart, make my heart like Your heart.*

The Woman Who Ordered the Peep Assassination was taking a nap on the couch. The Three Stooges were running the streets, as usual. The Italian Madman was not in his bed at his regular after-work nap time. Where could he be?

So I wrung out the mop really well, stood it up against the shingled wall in the yard, and went spying on him.

When I found him, he was standing two houses up the alley, glaring at the barking dog that was jumping at him through the cyclone fence. So I finagled a way to look like I was hosing down all the rooster and chicken poop. I had a feeling he was up to no good.

He had something in his right hand. When he saw me spying on him, he told me to mind my own business.

The very next time I cut through the alley, I did not hear or even see the dog. During the Italian Madman's nap the next night, the dog did not bark. The Woman Who Ordered the Peep Assassination told me that the Italian Madman had given the forever-barking dog a big steak with rat poison on it. It seemed like rat poison was getting used in this house for everything except the rats.

That reminds me of the steak situation in the house. When I cooked three T-bone steaks, one was for the Italian Madman, one was for #1 Favorite Son, and one was for the Midigan. The Woman Who Ordered the Peep Assassination was sure to cut off the three fatty ends from their steaks for her dinner and mine. Not that I ever starved, but this King Farouk thing with Italian men had to go. Who died and left them boss? The Woman Who Ordered the Peep Assassination and I waited on them hand and foot. Gimme a break. #1 Italian Son and the Midigan never did chores on Saturday. The Italian Madman never lifted a finger. I scrubbed the bathroom, scrubbed and waxed the living room and dining room floors, scrubbed the kitchen floor and the outside granite steps, went to the Italian grocery store on the corner to get the order, and fed Thunder, our dog. I learned how to trim steak watching the brothers who owned this store trim the meat. All the men just came home when they were done running the streets and got fed and waited on.

Poor Thunder. He was never the same after the Italian Madman picked him up by his neck and choked him. He must have weighed 150 pounds. He was a purebred German shepherd that barked when people came to the door and was always licking you, lying down wherever you were, and just being your friend. It happened when the Italian Madman had hurt the Woman Who Ordered the Peep Assassination again.

The Italian Madman kicked the Woman Who Ordered the Peep Assassination with his pointy, black Italian-bar-around-the-corner shoe. Her shin bled and bled and bled. She cried out. That is when Thunder came to her rescue (I told you he was a good dog). He growled and jumped on the Italian Madman. No problem. The Italian Madman picked him up and kept strangling him. I thought Thunder would die; later, I wished he had. His eyes were rolling back, he was making funny throat noises (like the Woman Who Ordered the Peep Assassination when the Italian Madman was strangling her on the toilet), and hair was sticking up all over his body; he even did a number two on the floor.

Then the Italian Madman just dropped him to the floor and walked away. Thunder slunk away with all four of his legs scrunched up underneath him, and he never barked at anybody or anything ever again. I tried to pay more attention to him in between school, church, the neighborhood, and just plain craziness all the time in the house. He did not make eye contact, and he dipped his head down low when you brushed your hair or raised your hand to pet him. My Thunder had lost his thunder.

Meanwhile, Favorite Aunt up the Street had shot Favorite Uncle up the Street again for some reason. He always managed to take care of his wounds himself. That omertà loyalty thing that Italian men had was crazy stuff. So he never dimed on her. Italian men can really keep quiet when they have to. Most other times, they never shut up.

When I finally went to bed, totally exhausted from school, preparing dinner, helping #1 Italian Son and the Midigan with their homework, writing excuse absence letters for my cousins up the street, and doing my own homework, the Italian Madman had had his nap and was back from the Italian bar around the corner, and now it was time to torture the Woman Who Ordered the Peep Assassination. Are you kidding me? Another all-nighter. I prayed, hummed out loud, put the pillow over my head, knelt on the floor, got under the bed, opened the window, put the fan on high, rolled myself up in my bedspread really tightly like Grandmom down the Alley told me they did to her when she was a baby, and tried to wake up #1 Italian Son.

I sneaked downstairs, got garlic, and put it in my undershirt, between my toes, and in my socks. If Dracula was afraid of it, maybe the Italian Madman would be would be too. What was I thinking? He ate it every night in his tomato salad. Nothing worked. I was up half the night and got to start all over again in the morning. I wanted to cry, I wanted to run away, I wanted to disappear. No waterworks were allowed in this house.

If the Italian Madman saw me crying, I would never hear the end of it. I was not allowed to shed any tears, ever. He called them crocodile tears. I wanted so badly to be waterlogged with tears and sink to the bottom of the Atlantic Ocean with all the other bottom dwellers. Every day in every way, living in that house was hard. Doing my chores, feeding the dog (trying to pay special attention after the strangulation event), feeding the cat, feeding the fish, looking for the snake that disappeared in the house, checking on the turtle, feeding the chickens and the roosters, watching that they did not come in contact with lye soap, and—God forbid—trying to sleep at night. That was the worst. Trying to sleep at night when he was keeping her up arguing, daring her to hit him, hurting her whether she did or didn't. No wonder she became an expert on rat poison.

So here I was, trying to be a kid and not having any luck. I was so excited one night when she cooked and didn't make Italian food. It was beautiful. I had never seen anything like it before. A whole platterful of pink ham (not the lunch meat ham) and green cabbage (not broccoli rabe) seasoned with bay leaves. She had cooked it in her new pressure cooker. I needed a break, and tonight I was getting one.

#1 Italian Son, the Midigan, and I sat quietly at the blue teapot table waiting to be served by the Woman Who Ordered the Peep Assassination. We could not wait to eat the pink and green food. We were so used to red food. Maybe that was what made him go off—the color.

The shed beside the kitchen was so cold all the time; that's where our dogs had their puppies. The Italian Madman let a dog in there once with Thunder and then closed the kitchen door and the back door so the two dogs had no way out. After a while, they were making screech sounds that sounded like they were coming from the movie *The Fly* I saw at the movie theater. Were they mixing atoms like the scientist in the movie? Would a fly that might be in the room end up with the head of a German shepherd dog and the German shepherd dog end up with the head of the fly? They were kind of like tin-scraping-on-tin sounds. "Help me. Help me."

So I peeked in and saw that they were end to end and had a pink, wet, hard thing stuck between the two of them, and they could not separate from each other. It did not look good. It reminded me of the pictures of ladies and men from the Italian Madman's picture book under the linoleum in his bedroom. Did they come in contact with Grandmom Up the Street's lye soap? Were they peeing and making babies? Did they eat the rat poison in the old Maxwell House coffee can on the shed floor?

We sat down to eat all excited, and the Italian Madman picked up the platterful of the pink and green Irish food, walked two steps to the shed, opened the door, and threw it in. The food splattered all over the attached German shepherds, the floor, and the walls. Are you kidding me? We were hungry. The platter broke in a million little pieces. Then he just walked away. I got the feeling he was making a statement. Was it the Italian thing again? It sure smelled good; we never even tasted it, but I got to clean it up.

Perfect attendance was easy. No way was I staying in this house any longer than was necessary.

Headache?

"It's only in your head; go to school."

Sore throat?

"It's only in your head; go to school."

I kept busy. I prayed my rosary, went to church, said my prayers and aspirations, fasted, and observed Lent. I kept reading all the time, going to the convent to escape, and in general, making like Casper the Friendly Ghost. The Woman Who Ordered the Peep Assassination was mad because I did not stick around on Sundays (when she cooked) so she could teach me how to make homemade macaroni. Favorite Cousin took my place. I could never live this one down.

I was on the second floor, and I could feel the floor vibrating. Not a good sign. I crept down the stairs, trying not to be noticed, and out the front door I went, leaving the Woman Who Ordered the Peep Assassination to fend on her own this time and feeling guilty about it. I heard the language, and it wasn't pretty.

"You are nothing but a f—— c——!" the Italian Madman screamed at her.

It was summer. Even though we were not allowed to do servile work on Sunday, I had done a load of wash and hung it on the line in the backyard that morning. It smelled so fresh when I hung it on the line. I knew a fight would ensue.

I transformed into the Flash, running very fast out the back door, under and through the laundry, pulling some of it down to the cement ground as I ran with superhuman speed. I looked back on the rest of the laundry swinging in the warm breeze as I made my escape around to the convent with the nuns. I could hear the Italian Madman cursing and screaming all our family's dirty laundry out loud for all the neighbors to hear. It was summertime, and the windows were wide open.

Attempting to manage two small children and an abusive husband, the mother thought she would lose her mind. The little girl stayed with her grandmother a lot those days. And the mother, when she felt strong enough after a beating, would call the police to come save her from this bully she married. The day after a beating, the mother paid a lot of attention to the abusive husband and tried to get him to love her.

The little girl felt confused.

4

Onion

I just wanted to escape. That is what made sense to me. The nuns wanted me to be one of them. When I was fourteen years old, I thought that was a great idea. I escaped to the convent every chance I got. The creepy, new-nun evaluation psychiatrist gave me all those Rorschach inkblots to describe. My encyclopedia said they were used to test emotions and personality.

I saw the man who came around the neighborhood sharpening knives and scissors in the inkblots. I heard the Saturday morning huckster singing, "Ehi! Banano nuovo! Ehi! Banano nuovo!" In one inkblot, I smelled my bedroom set burning (more on this later). I tasted the green and pink food I never got to taste before it hit the shed floor. In one inkblot, I saw me cleaning away the blood from the Woman Who Ordered the Peep Assassination's shin after the Italian Madman had kicked her with his pointy, black Italian-bar-around-the-corner shoe.

One inkblot made me breathless. It was the Italian Madman strangling Favorite Aunt up the Street for coming to help the Woman Who Ordered the Peep Assassination after he had beat her. Inkblots are not fun things. They made me remember, see, hear, and smell, taste, and feel real-life past, unhappy life events. They even had the power to take my breath away.

When the psychiatrist told me to keep quiet, I asked him why. He kept telling me that I needed to take orders and be passive. I was not going there. I did not need another wannabe *padrone* ordering me around and telling me what to do. The Italian Madman had already filled that job position.

Leave it to Italian Catholics in charge to make a way of life where women who always obeyed the men look good. The nuns always looked pressed. They told me they did not iron their habits; they just folded them when they took them off at night and put them between the mattress and the box spring. I made a note to try that. I would put my navy-blue Catholic school uniform under the mattress so I would not have to iron it in the morning before school. The beanie I would leave at the bottom of the bed, since I did not have a bureau anymore.

It seemed to me like the Woman Who Ordered the Peep Assassination's main goal in life besides getting me to make *homemades* was to get me to eat onion. She just did not get it. The taste wasn't bad; I liked the onion. The problem was that the onion did not like me. A nun wrote in my autograph book:

Life is an onion
You weep as you peel it

No weeping in this house; we were not allowed. I wish life were like ice cream instead. I wish life were sweet and made you feel good. Not like onion that made you cry a gallon of tears just peeling it. The kind of bowel situation it put me in after I ate it we will not even mention here. Let's just say I probably would not need a physic for a year.

I work hard at school and especially hard at home. My Irish friend up the street told me that her mother lined her up with her six siblings, and then the mother washed their hair, and the father cut their nails. In my house, kids did not line up and get waited on like this unless they were of the male gender. I washed the Italian Madman's Pontiac Star Chief (paying special attention to the gadgets inside, especially the ashtray), saddle-soaped his leather coat, went to the store to get his Marlboro cigarettes and Gillette double-edged razor blades, and polished his pointy, black Italian-bar-around-the-corner shoes.

The Italian Madman beat the Woman Who Ordered the Peep Assassination, and now there are marathon beatings of #1 Italian Son in the kitchen. When you are cornered into a friend from grade school coming over, you listen at the front door and put your hand flat on the outside of the door to feel for vibrations before attempting to go in. Screaming-beating-craziness sounds make vibrations on the wooden front door even if you cannot hear them. He called me Veronica Lake because my hair was always in my face. I wanted to love him, but I was afraid of him. He did not realize that with my new hairdo, I was trying to hide from him.

I escaped from the house and the neighborhood. I called the local radio station all the time and won tickets to go see Elvis Presley movies. I had the number for the transit authority memorized in my head: DA 9-4800. I even talked to a deejay from my favorite station one night and tried to tell him, without telling him (yep, I had inherited the omertà thing) about the family situation. He did not know what to say; I understood. The situation made me speechless sometimes too.

I escaped to visit my old sixth-grade nun who had been transferred from my parish to a suburb far away. Three different transfers were needed for this trip. I did not care. Public transportation was my way out. I wanted to travel to Asia and work with Tom Dooley, which is a hard thing to do when you are only a kid. Tom Dooley stole a line from the Our Father when he wrote his book *Deliver Us from Evil*. Be careful, Tom. You don't need any more aggravation than you already have. If Sister finds out, she will get you for copying, even if you are a doctor doing corporal works of mercy.

The nuns at my grade school always welcomed me in. I dusted, swept, scrubbed the convent, washed Our Lady's shrines in the convent backyard and in the first-floor alcove of the school, and went to the store for them. I made my own water course to the convent.

The nuns gave me temporary safe passage. I was a water beetle using my hind legs, swimming to the convent in the storm. When I bought the wrong thing, I needed to go back on the trolley (using another token), go back to the store, tell them my tale of woe, and bring the right thing right back to the convent.

"Take that chicken back, you nincompoop. Tell the chicken man to remove *all* the feathers, not just some of them. And get me three bunches of garlic."

Back on the trolley. Anything was better than being home. They played beautiful music in the convent, talked to each other nicely, and were calm. They even gave me an occasional piano lesson. I wished they were that calm in the classroom. The nun in second grade hung my friend out the second-story classroom window by his feet, and one smacked me when I filled her accordion water cup with water and it collapsed when I put it on her desk. It saturated all her school papers and her role book. Terror at school, terror at home.

One night, the house was very quiet. I fell asleep reading *The Agony and the Ecstasy*. I dreamed about #1 Italian Son and me. We stood facing each other. A big, heavy cord ran from around his feet to my waist. Every time I tried to move, I couldn't, and every time he tried to move, he tripped. We both had gigantic swords in our right hands, and we began to chop simultaneously at the middle of the heavy cord in between us.

I struggled to be free of the heavy cord, and after a lot of work, I stepped free of it. #1 Italian Son stepped clear of his heavy cord and went flying off in an upward direction. As he few upward, he turned and looked down at me. Then he tapped his heart several times. We were both silent. I nodded my head and tapped my own heart in response. We had passed a message between us, but no words were spoken.

The Irish lady up the street called #1 Italian Son a demon. I looked it up; it meant evil spirit. That was hitting him below the belt. He went to church and said his prayers; he tried to get his homework right; he was the Italian Madman's major contender who refused to fight back. These were boxing rounds that were one-sided with no one-minute breaks and no neutral corners. #1 Italian Son was born with a good chin and always stayed on his feet. Even when he got kicked with the pointy Italian-bar-around-the-corner shoes (personal foul), he stayed standing. If there was a referee, he would have called a lot of intentional fouls. Even I could recognize what I saw:

Hitting an opponent below the navel ...

Hitting an opponent when he is knocked down ...

Kicking ...

Use of abusive language ...

One nun was always calling me out of class to watch her beat him. He was beaten at home, and he was beaten at school. Then they had the nerve to wonder why the poor guy had an attitude some of the time. He helped old ladies cross the street; he rescued the Negro boys when the white kids attacked them at the high school. The nun smacked him over and over again in the hall—all haymakers. #1 Italian Son had proved he could go the distance. Somebody needed to report this nun to the boxing commission.

The only escape was public transportation. I am lying here; the real escape was reading. I read everything, all the time. I read the *Inquirer*. I read the *Bulletin*. I read *Moby Dick,* another story about a madman (not an Italian one). I read *Lust for Life* and *The Good Earth*. I even read *Chex Press* on the back of Rice Chex boxes that looked just like a newspaper. Reading saved me. I read the menu in the cheesesteak shop, the ingredients on food labels, pamphlets in the church vestibule, and matchbook covers. I learn a new word: a *phillumenist* is a person who collects matchbook covers.

I ran down to my locker in high school at lunchtime and read as much as I could of *Gone with the Wind*. Scarlett O'Hara was always taking care of crazy family business, always getting the short end of the stick. Kind of like me.

I took a recipe out of the Woman Who Ordered the Peep Assassination's *Betty Crocker's Good and Easy Cookbook* for vegetable beef soup with bay leaf in it, and I was planning on making it that night. It said that cabbage may be added. I would not do that for safety's sake. Everything else in the recipe could pass for Italian.

Life was just not fair. Life was especially not fair to the Woman Who Ordered the Peep Assassination and to #1 Italian Son, but parts of my world that I could escape to were good. My reason for escaping the neighborhood and my house was watertight, and I was a guilty, drowning mess. We played in the fireplug, and we stuck our backsides up against the opening where the forceful water gushed out. Our backsides forced huge arcs of water high in the air and saturated every car and every person that dared to cross the fireplug's path. Some grown-ups worked with us; one grown-up always had a wrench to open the fireplug. When the police came and shut it off, we just waited until they drove away, and an adult would get the wrench and open the fireplug again. We never dimed on the adult. Life was a never-ending water supply.

When I swam at the pool, I felt free. In the water, I felt weightless. We used to play a game and pull the drain cover off the drain at the bottom of nine feet. One time, I went down to the drain at the bottom of nine feet, holding my breath the whole time, and stuck my hand out to grab the cover. The third and fourth fingers of my right hand got stuck in the cover. My life flashed before my eyes. I was being buried with the fishes because I had dimed on someone, somewhere. I said an Act of Contrition and a rosary in about one minute. I could not hold my breath any longer, so I pulled my right hand back really hard to free it. I saw the red blood, bright at first, then watered down and pink in the water. When I swam to the top of nine feet again, no one had noticed I was gone.

I was wrong.

The Italian Madman, on the other side of the cyclone fence, had watched the whole deal, and he signaled me to get out of the pool. I followed him home and got ready for another belt beating. But this time, it didn't happen. I wish I knew why. I was beaten the least; Jesus was in my corner. I tried to figure it out, and I couldn't.

I felt grateful and guilty at the same time—more *G* words to add to the list.

The Woman Who Ordered the Peep Assassination had broken bones and a ruptured spleen. She had a half-inch-deep crater—she let me measure it one time—on her right shin (we called it the Italian-bar-around-the-corner crater). #1 Italian Son had a broken nose and black eyes. He was like Floyd Patterson in the ring with Sonny Liston—a real mismatch; #1 Italian Son didn't stand a chance. The Italian Madman, just like Sonny Liston, was bigger than his contender, and he weighed more. He was a bad boy with strength that could not be rivaled by #1 Italian Son, who was now over six feet tall and who chose not to hit his father.

I pictured myself and #1 Italian Son as Kirk Douglas and Tony Curtis in *Spartacus*. I was Spartacus, and they would never break my spirit. And I would kill Antoninus (#1 Italian Son) so that he could not be hurt ever again by any of them, especially the Italian Madman.

I dreamed of a wishing well that night when I went to sleep. I was standing near it and throwing in it all my Mallo Cup rewards. They stayed on the top of the water in the well and then became waterlogged and sank to the bottom. Since I could not see the bottom of the well, I asked my guardian angel, Desiree, to make sure they all landed on the bottom of the well faceup. It mattered how they landed if you got your wish or not. I wished again and again that the Italian Madman would stop beating my brother.

The baby boy grew up to be a wild, strong, handsome man. The mother, trying to amuse the little girl (now a young woman), would tell her stories of how her abusive husband had to be removed bodily from Pennsylvania Hospital on the day that the woman gave birth to the little girl. So greatly disappointed was he that the baby girl was just that—a girl and not a boy—he had acted out fiercely in the hospital and was verbally abusive to the mother, who was nursing the baby girl wrapped in her arms in the hospital bed.

The grown-up little girl felt unloved.

5

Celery

He was suddenly strangling me as I came down the stairs from the second floor; he was holding my body up against the wall by my neck. He was breathing so close to my face that I could feel the warmth and the spit of his garlic breath. He was using me to weaken her and water her down. Only I was at the end of the water runoff, and the force of the water was drowning me. She was on the stairs begging him to let me go, and he wouldn't. So what did she do?

She passed us on the stairs and upped the ante by going to get his gun.

Now she was pointing the gun at him, holding him at bay, telling him to let me down or she would shoot him. Was the Woman Who Ordered the Peep Assassination totally nuts?

"And whata you gonna do if I don't let her down?"

"You are chickenshit; you ain't gonna do a goddamn thing."

Why was he bringing that up here? Jaffe still loomed in my brain and crowded up my heart. I could suddenly hear the ending words of my old favorite TV show playing loudly in my brain as I pictured the Italian Madman shot dead and bleeding on the parquet floor.

There are eight million stories in the Naked City.

This has been one of them.

So she pulled the trigger. I was free; he was killed instantly from a single, close-range bullet wound right between his bushy eyebrows. But just to make sure, I waited a half hour and then called the police.

Only that was not the way it really went down. The gun misfired, and I dropped to the floor as he went after her to give her the beating of her life at the bottom of the first-floor stairs, just for trying to save me. The problem was that I had to do the right thing. I was just like the native Friday in *Robinson Crusoe*. Just the way Friday owed Robinson Crusoe for saving his life, I now owed a life debt to the Woman Who Ordered the Peep Assassination for saving mine.

Wow! Now that I am thinking about it, the native Friday and Detective Joe Friday have the same last names! Were they related? I did not have time to ponder that now. (I memorized the synonyms for ponder — think, reflect, consider.) The Woman Who Ordered the Peep Assassination was being beaten to a pulp at the bottom of the first-floor stairs for saving my life.

And I couldn't call the police; the two of them were in the way of the phone. He caught me watching him beat her, and the mind racing, blocked vision, heart trying to jump out of my chest, rooted in one spot, can't-breathe deal returned. I developed a name for it—the SSS, "scared shitless syndrome." My Paulie the Junkman dictionary said that a syndrome is a set of things happening at the same time; that form a pattern. I could figure this pattern out; it was getting to be a regular.

He sent me upstairs. I didn't know whether I should take the steps by twos or threes (14 steps ÷ 2 = 7 jumps, 14 steps ÷ 3 = 4 2/3 jumps). The two-thirds is too hard to figure out with the SSS going on, so I just jumped the steps three at a time. Of course, I was the only one home with the two of them going at it again. I was screaming out loud, only I was calling underwater at the bottom of the ocean, so no one could hear me.

I thought again of Hilts (Steve McQueen) throwing that baseball in *The Great Escape*. My house was a stalag, I was a prisoner, and it was my duty to try to escape. But how could I do it? I knew one thing: now that I owed the Woman Who Ordered the Peep

Assassination a life debt, I could not escape until she was safe. I could get the old Italian sodality ladies who sang in church on Sunday to sing out loud and be our cover while we escaped. I looked out the window at the back of the house that faced the alley. I tried calling to several Negro men I saw fighting with each other in the alley.

I remember one time running home to ask the Woman Who Ordered the Peep Assassination why we got smacked in the mouth if we even tried to say the *N* word. Here were two Negro men calling each other that name!

"Because they are allowed to say that word. You are not."

Now he had chased her into the backyard. I could see them clearly from my stance at the window, and I made my getaway. I crept down the stairs and got to the phone.

"Hello, this is … I live at … my father is beating my mother again."

Busted again.

He had doubled back into the house and caught me as I uttered the last syllable, and he threw me across the room. Then I really escaped. I went to the convent to be with the nuns. It was Sunday. The Woman Who Ordered the Peep Assassination could go ahead and call Favorite Cousin to make homemades with her. I had stepped over the warning wire, and I was free for now. I would have to owe her for saving my life another time.

Guns were part of the scenery. I was cleaning #1 Italian Son's bedroom on the second floor (we graduated to our own rooms; I chose the bedroom next to the scimitar room on the third floor [stay tuned for more on this later], the farthest away from you know who), and I was using the dust mop. As I bent down to mop under the bed, I heard this *crack-pop* sound. So I lifted my body up and looked around. I climbed on top of the bed and looked around.

And guess what I saw?

A hole in the window that happened to be in a direct line with a hole in the ceiling, and both of these holes happened to be in line with the street where Grandmom down the Alley lived. No surprise there. A bullet is lodged in the ceiling. If I were standing up straight at the time, I would have caught a bullet in the head.

The people on the back street where Grandmom down the Alley lived were neat. Favorite Cousin lived with Grandmom down the Alley, and she and I loved the people. They played music, danced outside, and straightened their hair on the front steps by running in and out of the house with the curling iron that heated up on the gas stove.

So one day, I was waiting in line; I wanted my nappy hair straightened too.

"What is the matta with all y'all eye-talian people? You always smells like garlic. Onions is good too; can't you switch it up once in a while?"

I did not want to explain to the Negro girl ahead of me in the sidewalk line that it was an Italian Dracula thing. I thought only Italian people could understand that.

"Whatsa matta fah you? You craz?"

There she was, always nabbing you, good old Grandmom down the Alley.

"Thatsa nota fah you. You Italiana. That's a why you sucha gooda gal. You eata the ends of the Italian bread; it a makea your hair a curly."

So there I was, doomed to a lifetime of nappy hair. Favorite Aunt up the Street sang a song to me when I was little:

Your hair is nappy.
Who is your pappy?
You some ugly child.

The Italian Madman used to take us down the cellar to practice shooting. Put a wooden clothespin on the spout of a glass half-gallon milk bottle and then aim and shoot. I got perfect aim by pretending the head of the clothespin was his head. Clothespin after clothespin went down. Then we would all be free.

Just like the time a person who did not live in the neighborhood stole Grandmom down the Alley's portable TV—the one Poppy used to watch *The Price Is Right* in the kitchen. Two of my aunts went to the back street and started shooting guns in the middle of the street, not aimed at any particular target.

Then they went into Grandmom down the Alley's house and tore it apart with hammers and hatchets. They made a big deal of taking all her food out of the icebox and throwing it in the middle of the street. Small kids on the block made a game out of catching the onions as they rolled down the skinny blacktop street. I watched a car run over the stalk of celery and squash it like the grasshoppers and Favorite Cousin and I experimented on (more on this later).

"We can't move Mommy's stuff," they decreed. "And the people on this street ain't getting it."

Anything in their black-water path went down. There were no watermarks on Grandmom down the Alley's furniture. It was old but in perfect condition. She had it since she had come to America in 1929. She was my precious water gem, and water rats were trying to drown her. Their actions held Grandmom down the Alley at bay, and she could not retreat; she could not go forward. The police did not come very often on Grandmom down the Alley's street. The people on this street were either very good in the policemen's eyes or they were ignored. I wish I had Wyatt Earp's phone number. We needed a lawman to take care of this matter. The police were not coming.

Then they moved Grandmom down the Alley to a second-floor apartment on their street. Were they non compos mentis? Were they bumps on the same log? The problem was that Grandmom down the Alley could not go up and down steps now. The doctor visited the house not long ago and said she had emphysema. The little lady with a big bump on her back who had tried to save me fifty million times needed a way out.

So I taught her to use the phone.

I made her a telephone address book out of construction paper squares and the shoelaces that she used to tie everything up with. She couldn't read, but she could recognize numbers. I translated all the telephone exchanges—GR, TR, SA—into numbers. I glued a picture of the person onto the construction paper squares and wrote the person's phone number in a column beside it. Everyone she loved or wanted to call had their own construction paper square. She got it right the first time. It worked like a charm.

For a week.

Within a week, I was getting cursed out by the Woman Who Ordered the Peep Assassination and my aunt who lived on the same street as Grandmom down the Alley (who now lived around the corner). Let's keep her original name of Grandmom down the Alley for the sake of clarity (I heard Sister say this and wrote it in my copy book; it means *the state of being clear*). Grandmom down the Alley was now calling them to death.

"Why in the hell did you have to teach her how to use the phone? Now she calls us every time she needs something."

I wanted to say, "No shit, Sherlock. That's the general idea here."

Of course, I did not curse; I did not want to add cursing to the long list of sins I already had to confess on Saturday. How did they expect her to get groceries, feed Poppy, feed herself, *live*? They wanted to throw me in the cooler, but I was too smart for that. Steve McQueen and I had made a pact long ago; I was the new cooler king and mentally would just keep bouncing that baseball against the wall until I could make an escape.

The English teacher told us to write a descriptive essay from someone else's point of view. I chose the Midigan. He hardly ever spoke except to #1 Italian Son, so I figured something needed to be said from his point of view. I chose the scimitar incident, because I still felt bad about his broken front teeth from when he fell down the stairs.

An Innocent Man's Story

I was making holes in the plaster wall on the third floor with a long sword. It was a curved sword. My foster sister looked it up in her dictionary or her encyclopedia; it is called a scimitar. She was always looking up things in her stupid, fat dictionary and in the stupid, skinny *Encyclopedia Britannica* books. My foster brother was doing it too; we were taking turns. He is my best friend in the whole, wide world. Then I heard my creepy foster sister coming up the stairs. She was always hollering at us (she was always hollering at us for something) to stop. She must have heard us from downstairs; we were making a lot of racket.

Always telling us what to do. Who died and left her boss? So what? We were making big holes in the back bedroom wall. Who would find out? Nobody ever went up there, anyway. Only her. Her bedroom was on the third floor. I got her number; it was probably the farthest she could go to get away from the rest of us.

So she kept begging us to stop. We could not listen to her anymore. We never listen to her, anyhow. My foster brother and I were having a ball. Plaster chunks from the wall were flying all over the place; the floor was covered with them, and we were breathing in the plaster powder in the air. She tried to grab the sword out of my hand (my foster brother and I were taking turns stabbing the wall, like I said, and it was my turn), and I wouldn't let her.

We just kept laughing and stabbing, stabbing and laughing, and we were making loud Tarzan yells as we stabbed the wall. She tried to push my foster brother out of the room, and he was too big, so he did not budge. She started pushing me out of the room, and I was pushing her right back. We ended up in the hallway at the top of the third-floor stairs.

Before I knew it, I was flying down the stairs. She probably didn't mean to push me down. She gets on my nerves and bosses us around all the time (my foster brother and our cousin and me) when she is the only one home. I landed at the bottom of the stairs, and my front two teeth were broken. My mouth felt hot and tasted of salty fluid. I don't know why, but I started running to the yard. I was leaving a trail of Hawaiian punch fruit-juicy blood all over the floor as I ran.

My foster sister was coming after me, crying, and she looked scared to death.

When Mommy came home, and she told Mommy what happened, Mommy turned on her. It made me think about my foster sister's favorite movie, *Gone with the Wind*, when Mammy says to Scarlett, "You know what trouble I's talkin' 'bout. I's talkin' 'bout Mr. Ashley Wilkes. He'll be comin' to Atlanta when he gets his leave, and you sittin' there waitin' for him just like a spider."

Mommy never paid attention to her, only when she needed her to do something or to take care of us. I got my teeth capped.

My foster sister was always with the nuns at the convent. My foster brother and I couldn't care less about the nuns, and the feeling was mutual. We always watch *The Rocky and Bullwinkle Show* together, my foster sister and me. If this story was an Aesop fable, I would say that the moral of this story is let it go, foster sister, let it go.

Because the little girl inside the grown woman knew fear, abandonment, and confusion so well, she chose a husband who perpetuated those feelings inside her. She thought that these crazy feelings stirred up inside her heart meant that he loved her.

She felt lost.

6

Carrot

So we fly (synonyms—flit, hover, wing, glide, soar, dart) around the corner, #1 Italian Son and I. We stopped and bought a book at Paulie the Junkman's garage. We always got good deals there. Last week, we finagled him down to twenty-five cents for a ten-pound *Webster's* dictionary. You couldn't beat it! I was the "good one" in school, and #1 Italian Son was the bad seed, the one the nuns slapped around (yep, I saw the movie *The Bad Seed*—the mother had used sleeping pills on her own kid, but the pills didn't work, just like rat poison doesn't work sometimes).

#1 Italian Son would never use this dictionary; it would be all mine. Some library threw this book out. Were they nuts? But Paulie the Junkman had rescued it from the deep. I pictured Paulie, the neighborhood frogman, swimming to the bottom of the Atlantic Ocean, a regular Lloyd Bridges in *Sea Hunt*, wrestling the book from the tentacles of an octopus (eight tentacles—I figured it out: *octo* means "eight"; I did my homework) and then swimming back to the neighborhood.

I wondered if the percentage of water in Paulie's body changed after his ocean book retrieval? If he were my science project in school (good luck with this one; we hardly ever did science in Catholic school), I could measure the amount of water in his body. I would lay him down on a rubber cot, and on his hands and feet, I would put electrodes (I could get Favorite Cousin to mind the store for him; she was a good right-hand man, especially when we experimented on grasshoppers ... more on this later, I swear).

Then I would then put gel on him (I could use Dippity-Do) and run electricity through his body. Of course, we didn't want to kill the guy; he was on our favorite expedition list for when things got boring, so we would use a low current—around 50 kHz. I would expect the water level in his body to be high since he had just been at the bottom of the Atlantic Ocean. I was puzzled and could not figure out whether, since the ocean was salty, he would be really thirsty after the swim. Would his skin shrivel up like Sosabet, the old Italian lady up the street? Would he have more water inside his cells or outside?

I knew we would have to be really careful with this experiment if we did it in the cellar. Maybe I could ask permission and the nun would let us do it as a science experiment in the classroom. I did not want rescuers on the Atlantic Ocean to get confused, as the encyclopedia said that 2,182 kHz is also the international distress frequency for people who need to be rescued on the ocean. Yep, we would play it safe at 50 kHz—even though, if they came to our school by mistake on a saving expedition, they could save a few of us from the clutches of the nun who hung us by our feet out the second-story window (the same nun who slapped me in the face when her accordion water cup collapsed on her desk).

I was learning about the goddess Artemis in school. It was her job to protect and kill animals. That's what I called the accordion-cup sister—Sister Artemis. Funny thing, she didn't look that strong, but she had the ability to turn into the goddess Artemis on a dime; I pictured her with a bow and arrow. Come to think of it, one time, Favorite Cousin and I were playing in the alley near Grandmom down the Alley's yard when we saw a lion a block away at the end of the alley. We were terrified. We didn't even think of calling on Sister

Artemis; she could have shot the lion with her bow and arrow. At the time, I wasn't sure if Desiree did lion duty.

So we ran into Grandmom down the Alley's kitchen and screamed at the top of our lungs that there was a lion in the alley.

"Mah, whatta you craz? The lion she is ina the zooa and ina Africa, the lion she isa nota in the alley."

Maybe the lion was taking a vacation from the zoo. Maybe he didn't like the food. Maybe he wanted to be free like I did. When we went back to check, the lion was gone. Sometimes we wished Sister would be gone too. If we could talk her into holding up the world for Atlas like Hercules did, she might be too busy, and she would leave us alone.

She didn't look that strong, and I knew one day she would not be able to hold on and would drop one of us on our heads out the window. So I would keep 2,182 kHz in my bag of tricks in case I needed it to rescue one of us in the classroom later on.

And who needed saving more than Saint Sebastian? I looked him up in the encyclopedia under *martyr*. A salesman brought encyclopedia books right to our front door—a life miracle. Sister taught us about martyrs in school. A martyr is one who dies for something he believes in. Saint Sebastian was a martyr. I wanted to be a martyr if it meant I was going to heaven, but I didn't want to suffer. Poor Saint Sebastian! A martyr could really be a mess. He had fifty million arrows sticking out from all over his body. Saint Sebastian loved Jesus, so the Romans did not love him. I knew he had to be Italian. I cogitated (synonyms—contemplated, considered) which arrow had finished the job. Probably the one near his heart. No fair! He couldn't even fight back; they had him tied to a tree.

The Woman Who Ordered the Peep Assassination was cooking her version of chicken cacciatore. I could smell the garlic, bay leaf, and onion. Last time I looked in on her (she was safe; the Italian Madman was not home yet), she asked me to chop up the celery and carrot, which I did, and I left them on the sideboard of the sink.

A little while later, I heard chopping going on in another part of the house. The Italian Madman was chopping up the bedroom set that his friend had given me that I loved. It had a vanity where I sat every night and put Lady Esther cold cream on my face and wrapped strands of my hair in toilet paper rolls to straighten them—or with Spoolies if I wanted my hair curled in a smooth (not nappy) way. Of course, Dippity-Do (the strong green one) helped too.

No clue about what upset him this time.

We were learning how to do expository writing in English class, and I was glad for three reasons; I will put the reasons in order building up to the most important.

1. He did not chop up the bed, and I still could use it to sleep in.
2. He wasn't chopping up one of us.
3. This deal was on him, and I didn't have to confess it on Saturday.

He made me help him bring the ragged pieces of wood down from my third-floor bedroom to the coal stove in the basement. We took turns throwing in pieces of wood into the stove and watching them burn. I imagined Detective Joe Friday coming to the house. I would be the one answering the front door as usual.

"All we want are the facts, ma'am."

Why would a detective call me *ma'am*? What kind of excuse would the Italian Madman give him for chopping up a perfectly good bedroom set? What if I went to the Los Angeles Police Department where he worked and asked to speak to Joe Friday to give them the facts, and they told me it was Joe's day off? The Italian Madman would be executed in a manner prescribed by law.

No such luck.

My other Favorite Aunt up the Street told me once that Grandmom up the Street (the Italian Madman's mother) was very beautiful when she was young. A neighbor told my aunt that she remembered Grandmom up the Street coming into the neighborhood off the boat with her first baby in her arms, looking for her husband, the man who had left her pregnant in Italy when he got on the boat for America.

The neighbor said she was as beautiful as a flower with her dark black hair pulled all up on top of her head. How did she find her husband in a new country? She didn't care; she walked right through the spraying fireplug water with her baby in her arms. How rude was my grandfather up the street that he could not pick her up when she got off the boat on Ellis Island? How did she know her way in America and to the neighborhood? How did the baby in her arms not drown in the fireplug?

Sometimes I had to get my guts back before I went to see Grandmom up the Street. I felt like one of those scared cowboys I used to see on *The Adventures of Wild Bill Hickok*. The ones with rabies. They would tie them up and pour out a pitcher of water in front of them to torture them. When I looked at her at the kitchen sink making a stew with *baccala*, potatoes, tomatoes, bay leaf, onion, celery, and prunes, I was scared to say anything, and she was always acting like nothing was going on. I had experience with her; I knew that was not always the case.

I couldn't figure out if I was more afraid of her sometimes or of Ghost Town, which was what we named the part of the cemetery where we only went when it was dark outside. When I brought up the subject of Jaffe (yeah, Grandmom, *remember him?*), she acted like she did not understand.

"*No capisco*, Mommy, no capisco."

Why did Italian people call people they supposedly loved (and whose ducks they cooked) *Mommy*? Grandmom up the Street was always cooking. Boarders were living in every corner of her house, and she often made like the Invisible Man when she disappeared with an old Italian man into the vacant (synonyms—empty, unoccupied) house next door to us.

I envisioned the old Italian man taking off her bandages (just like the Invisible Man did in the movie) and the poor Italian man being shocked because he could not see her body. Then she would take all his money and leave him for dead. I would discover her footprints in the snow from when she escaped the crime scene. Another story for the Naked City.

One time when I was sitting on her front stoop, it started to rain, and the sun was so hot. How could it be raining when the sun was out and so hot? The neighborhood kids were playing in the fireplug. Then I noticed that the rain falling on me was yellow and coming in a single stream from Grandmom up the Street's third-floor window right down onto my shoulder. This was nuts. Was God punishing me with water like He did the Egyptians? Where was Moses when you needed him?

How could I part this stream of yellow water coming out of the third-floor window when it already looked thin? What was the deal? Was it a miracle in the making? It was Gaetano, one of Grandmom up the Street's boarders, saving himself a trip to the bathroom and peeing out the third-story front window. Gimme a break.

The next thing I knew, the Italian Madman caught Grandmom up the Street in the vacant house next to ours and beat up the old Italian man who was in there with her. The men statues in the art museum had leaves for private parts; was the old Italian man showing his leaf to Grandmom up the Street?

The Italian Madman pulled him outside, and the old man's head kept bouncing off the brick wall on the front of my house fifty million times as the Italian Madman delivered fifty million right jabs and gave him fifty million uppercuts. The round needed to end; it was lasting too long! I was trying to call it, and nobody was listening. It looked like a remake of the Cassius Clay–Sonny Liston fight. Yeah, the old man was strong and big, but the Italian Madman had the advantage of arm length and speed from what I could see. In my mind, I called a technical knockout.

There was at least a gallon of yucky blood on the bricks. Later, it was my job to hose it down and get rid of the evidence before the police came. Why were they trusting such an important job to a girl? Wasn't evidence important? Officer Friday would not care for the way this case was being handled. My other Favorite Aunt up the Street even told me that Grandmom up the Street was in the *Bulletin* once. She firebombed a house in the neighborhood for a reason nobody could ever figure out. The way I figured it, if she would have been nabbed and done time back then, she would never have been around to kill Jaffe. But then I would have never been born, either.

My grandfather Angelo up the street (alias the big mahoff) used to beat Grandmom up the Street all the time. I never met the big mahoff; he died the week before I was born. Maybe that is where the Italian Madman got the beating-women thing from. It was too late for the firebombed house. When the fire truck came, they did not even pull out their water hoses. The house was burned to a crisp, and there was no water pressure because of all the Italian kids playing in the fireplug.

Grandmom up the Street could not (and did not want to) read or write, but she could knit, crochet, sew, tat, make lye (duck-killer) soap, and stretch the doilies she made on a frame. And cook. Cooking was a way of life, her purpose in life, and the reason why she was born. She cooked for Max, the German husband she married for his pension (after the big mahoff died), for all her boarders, and for whoever walked into the house at the time. If Jesus fed five thousand people with seven loaves and a few fish, Grandmom up the Street fed twenty-five people with several trays of rice pudding.

When she made pies, she made *pies*—and with no recipe. Roll up the crust, flop it in the pie pan. Pick peaches (I looked them up: *Prunus persica*) from the trees in the yard, cut them up, sprinkle cinnamon and sugar on top, put the pie in the oven. Make baccala stew. Soak the baccala; cut it up. There was a wine press in the basement right beside the vat of duck-killer lye soap she always cleaned the house with. She was not a Holy Roller, but on Sundays, she was always going to the cemetery across the street to sit at my uncle Danny's grave (her son who died at sixteen from tuberculosis).

I would spot-check her all the time. She would sit there and crochet for hours.

So there I was in the flesh, still trying to make sense, after all this time, out of the Jaffe thing, and she was not answering me. She just kept crocheting her doily. She was Poseidon, god of the sea, in her left hand a *trident* (crochet hook). Like Poseidon, when she was kind, she could do really good things (remember the peach pies and rice pudding?). When she was angry, get ready.

In my Greek mythology book, which I saved for special occasions on the weekend to read, it said that Alexander the Great, before the Battle of Issus, sent a chariot with four horses into the sea to die and drown as a sacrifice to Poseidon. Maybe the horse that the Italian Madman punched was a relative of one of those horses that drowned, and the horse didn't like the Italian Madman because he was a relative of Grandmom up the Street (Poseidon) who drowned his horse mommy or daddy. It made perfect mythical sense to me.

That day, she fooled me. The seas looked calm. I had no reason to expect a drowning or a shipwreck. Then she threw her crochet hook on the floor and told me to pick it up. On the floor next to the crochet hook was a huge, knotted clump of sewing string that she used to pull string from when she needed to sew. It was usually always on the end table.

Come to think of it, why did they call tables on the end of the couch *end tables*? They didn't call tables in front of the couch *front tables*? I was slowly getting the message; Grandmom Poseidon was up to something today.

"Mah, Mommy, you please a picka me upa my string on the floor."

As not doing a dry fig was not my style, I stooped to pick up the knotted clump from the floor for her. Why was it on the floor in the first place? Why did she throw her crochet hook on the floor near it? Probably to mark the place the way a male dog marks his place like when he pees on the fireplug. Was she having trouble bending and needed me to help her? I was obedient, her faithful water bearer, trying to find my individuality and stressing equality for all the girls in the world.

As I picked up the string, I noticed that it had red, wet, gooey stuff on it. There I was trying to figure out the gooey stuff when my eyes met up with Max, who was sitting in a chair in the corner across the room. Always kind. Always drunk. Today, he looked even more of a mess.

I remember looking up and back from my spot on the floor at Grandmom up the Street, who was sitting on the couch. I remember asking her, "Grandmom, what's this red, gooey stuff on your string?"

"Oh, that's a nothing, Mommy. Itsa justa Max's a hair."

This was not her thread on the floor; it was Max's hair that she pulled out of his head when she beat him right before I showed up on the scene. I wondered if she ever hit the big mahoff back years ago when he beat her. She was a sea force. She never said it, but I knew she loved me.

Maybe that is where the Italian Madman got the beating-people-up thing. The big mahoff beat Grandmom up the Street, Grandmom up the Street beat up Max, and the Italian Madman beat up the Woman Who Ordered the Peep Assassination and #1 Favorite Italian Son. It was a real family tradition.

While at work one day, the woman received a phone call that her brother, the wild, strong, handsome man that she loved so much, had been in a car accident and would probably soon die. How could he, who had been her partner through all the witnessed and actual beatings of their mother and himself, leave her here alone with them?

The little girl inside the woman attempted to communicate with the little boy inside the man who lay dying on the hospital bed. He told her that he loved her, and he hoped he had won the football game that put him here in the hospital. He died soon after with a respirator attached to his face. The little girl cringed at the dried blood on his teeth. The woman thought that the little girl inside her died with her brother on the bed.

The woman felt empty of all hope.

7

Parsley

Which brings me back to Grandmom down the Alley. It was always me and her when the Italian Madman went nuts; we were a team. I learned from the dictionary how to spell her back condition. I looked it up in Paulie the Junkman's dictionary: s-c-o-l-i-o-s-i-s. When she walked, she lifted her left foot higher than her right foot. Grandmom down the Alley seemed more of a scaredy-cat than Grandmom up the Street. She went to church all the time and carried her rosaries in the pocket of her housedress. One Tuesday, slop day, maggots captured her garbage can. The garbage can was overflowing with maggots onto the pavement.

Grandmom down the Alley knew the importance of water. She knew it could be life-giving *and* life-taking. She pulled out the hose from the cellar window and flooded the maggots down the pavement. Those maggots got baptized in a Jack-and-the-Beanstalk kind of way. They could only swim for so long, and then they were gone, floating off to maggot heaven (or hell, if they had a mortal sin on their maggot souls that they did not get a chance to confess). Come to think of it, if they had venial sins on their souls, they were off to maggot purgatory to do their time there. Their still-alive maggot friends who prayed for them could earn indulgences for them; I knew that would take care of their purgatory time. So no problem.

Grandmom down the Alley kept a pet rabbit, and I was commissioned to feed Bugsy carrots when he was hungry. I felt it was my responsibility to make sure that Grandmom up the Street never came in contact with Grandmom down the Alley's rabbit. For sure, the rabbit and any uncooked carrots Bugsy didn't eat yet would go into Grandmom up the Street's soup pot. I knew she had no morals when it came to animals that could be cooked. One day, Grandmom up the Street had a dead squirrel soaking in a pot of water in the kitchen. She would probably even ask me when I visited to throw in the bay leaf, onion, and celery, which she added to everything (even squirrel stew). No, thank you.

Grandmom down the Alley brought cures (memorized in her head) with her from Italy. When Favorite Cousin sprained her ankle (remember that she was always running the streets with #1 Italian Son and the Midigan?), Grandmom down the Alley made an ankle cast out of egg whites. When we had bad breath, Grandmom down the Alley made us chew on parsley. When we had a black-and-blue mark, she crushed up parsley leaves with water and put the mixture on our bruise. A regular Italian water witch.

The Woman Who Ordered the Peep Assassination always said that Grandmom down the Alley (her mother) could kill you with her tongue. I experienced that firsthand. When the Italian Madman beat the Woman Who Ordered the Peep Assassination, Grandmom down the Alley was the first on the scene, trying to kill the Italian Madman with her tongue, screaming in Italian at him.

Grandmom down the Alley was not much of a cook. A wonderful lunch was fried peppers, lightly salted, a loaf of crunchy Italian bread (we broke it with our hands), and iced tea with lemon, which was not very sweet. Once in a while, there was a baked chicken loaded with garlic. Sometimes she put pieces of celery on the table for us to munch. She cleaned her tiny row home until it was spit shined.

She made an order from the grocery store up the street, and they delivered.

"Mah, you sucha gooda gal," she told me all the time. "Read, you read. You be a bigga shot."

"I love you, Grandmom."

"Mah, I love a you! Getta me the boxa salt outa the closet and open a the light."

Grandmom down the Alley did not care that I was not a boy. I was her oldest grandchild. She loved me for me. She patted my nappy hair down, made me sit down and watch Lawrence Welk with her, and spoke to me in Italian. One tall green cabinet in her kitchen held all her dishes, pots, silverware, and bowls. She raised the Woman Who Ordered the Peep Assassination like this and three other daughters without two cents to her name.

She told me she even bootlegged for a while after my grandfather (her first husband from Italy) died from the pleurisy he got from a stab wound in the Italian bar up the street. She made whiskey to stay alive and keep her four daughters alive. She told me she went to the Catholic church one time and asked the priest for milk money for her children.

"I am a so sorry. The Church, she is a poor too," the priest lied.

And here's where the story gets really interesting. Not long after that, the priest in the "poor" church died and left $22,000 to his sister. Grandmom down the Alley never forgot that one.

"Mah, you somna bitch!" she said out loud when she heard he died and left all that money.

There you go again. Someone's mother was getting cursed out again for something her kid did. It did not seem fair. She stood at the kitchen sink, washing dishes, the spigot water running. Light from the skylight poured over her body. She was the goddess Nu, who controls all storms. She looked kind and peaceful, but the Woman Who Ordered the Peep Assassination and my aunts always tried not to go at it with her.

I was safe when I was with Grandmom down the Alley. Because

I looked like her, the Woman Who Ordered the Peep Assassination and her sisters were always treating me weirdly. They said I was her favorite. What was the deal? I was just like Sophia Loren, and they (my aunts) were the Catholic Church in Italy who did not want her married to Carlo Ponti. Because I always tried to help Grandmom down the Alley, they thought I was sucking up.

I bet Hester Prynne felt guilty all the time like me. Sure, I did not have to wear a scarlet capital *A* on my chest, but the feeling was always there. Grandmom down the Alley was always patting my head and squeezing my cheek. I understood where she was coming from. The crowd that life gave her to play to in America was tough. I never knew the priest who would not help her with milk money, but I gave him a name—Father Dimmesdale, the same name of the reverend in *The Scarlet Letter* who would not help out Hester and tell the truth about their baby, Pearl.

"You look like Grandmom," Favorite Cousin told me all the time.

"She is Grandmom's favorite," they all would agree.

"You have no idea what she was like when we were little."

But I did. They told me over and over, fifty million times. Grandmom would tell me to go out to the yard and pick the *vassanagol* (basil) for the tomato salad; then she would make a plain salad with tomatoes, fresh basil, garlic, vinegar, and oil. She never learned how to read and write. She never stopped telling me to read and write. She always spoke broken English. I learned how to understand some Italian by paying attention when she was saying things in Italian that she did not want me to know. It was hard to believe Grandmom down the Alley that I was "such a gooda gal." I did not feel good. I felt sinful. That's why I went to confession every week.

Poppy, her second husband, loved all of us. He had his medicine every morning before breakfast. He thought we kids did not know that his "medicine" was whiskey. He had it every morning right after he woke up, right before his coffee and chocolate Tastykakes—a package of them in the morning with his coffee and medicine, and he was set until lunchtime. He walked with a limp. He raised his right foot when he walked. When he and Grandmom down the Alley walked together up the street, he on the outside, she on the inside, they went up and down together, her raising her left foot, him raising his right foot, and they kind of made a peak in the center like a human seesaw if you were watching them from behind.

Poppy told me someone hit him over the head as a young man when he was working delivering ice as an ice man, and this caused him to be crippled. He told us stories of the Spanish-American War, of how the soldiers were given only water and a small muffin to eat. They were so hungry, tired, and thirsty all the time, and there was no water anywhere to get washed.

Poppy was always in a good mood. He loved Grandmom down the Alley. Favorite Cousin told me that Grandmom down the Alley did not want to marry Poppy at first, because she did not like his bald head. He was always putting his hands up her dress when he thought I did not see. From what I could tell, he never went to church or confession. You'd better think about confessing this one, Poppy.

"Noan you fight."

That was his advice to us all the time. Not to fight. How could you help but? Everyone was always arguing about something in my house.

Favorite Cousin knew how to jump double Dutch like she was born doing it. I just couldn't get the hang of it. All the neighborhood kids played jacks, Bucky Bucky Beaver, bottle caps, hide the belt, kick the can, pimple ball, pinball, pool (if you were old enough and Jessie in the pool room let you in), and throwing old sneakers over the telephone wires. If you had a date, you went to George's Hill in Fairmount Park to make out.

I was the big stoop at home babysitting, watching #1 Italian Son, Favorite Cousin, and the Midigan. I did a lot of cleaning and cooking like I was a Roman slave. I never learned how to play or had the time; I was the neighborhood egghead. When I did get a chance to go outside and play, I played school, and I was the teacher. I brought my schoolbooks out and taught all the kids on the block. I did not have many friends, and the one or two I did have I was afraid to bring home because anything could make the Italian Madman snap out.

I had just read about Cronus in my Greek mythology book. I so wanted to overthrow the Italian Madman as Cronus had overthrown his father, Uranus. But then the story goes that Cronus ate his kids so that they would not overthrow him. I totally did not want to eat my kids if I ever got out of the house alive and lived long enough to have them.

Words were my friends. I read Paulie the Junkman's *Webster's* dictionary from cover to cover. I was always looking up words like *aqueous* and *delusion* and learning how to spell and pronounce them. The nuns loved that I loved to read. So did Grandmom down the Alley.

I needed to write an essay for English class. English was hard, but words were not. When I did not have time to play outside or have friends, words were my friends. I decided on a reflective essay (synonyms—form an image, manifest, show). I did not know who or what I was, and I needed to help myself find out. I would use the analogy of a book and I would follow the format I found in my English book.

Title: I Am a Book

Introduction
    I do books. All my childhood life so far, I have done books. Nothing in the world can compare to a book. Chiang Kai-shek once said, "We become what we do." If that is true, then I am becoming a book.

Body

Paragraph 1

I love the look, feel, weight, words, pages, and the knowledge contained in a book. I started collecting pages in my book life when I was very young. My grandmother cannot read, and she makes sure she tells me in Italian every day to read. My father tries to read the *Philadelphia Bulletin,* and when he gets stuck on a word, he sends me to *Webster's Dictionary* to look it up. I love to use the tattered, ten-pound version of *Webster's Dictionary* that my brother and I purchased at Paulie the Junkman's for a quarter.

Paragraph 2

The pages in my life as a book have been adding up all my life—from first grade until now. There are so many pages! All the same, yet all different. I am the same person, yet I am reinvented every time I read a page in a book.

Paragraph 3

One day, I would like to write a book. Meanwhile, I will just keep adding more thoughts, feelings, and pages to myself, the book. I will keep adding more letters, words, phrases, sentences to myself. I will keep reading the words—they go inside me; they live there and never die. Everlasting words on everlasting pages in an everlasting book. As a book, I am an important part of my own private book club. Somehow, though, I feel I am only a visitor. Many others have critiqued me, the book. That is their option. Many do not have as many pages as I have, and they do not know. Others have more pages, and I can learn from them.

Conclusion

The book of my life is heavy right now, and I am trying to stay on the page. A bookshelf is a comfortable place to be for a book, and a bookmarker keeps me on track. I am home.

I just loved books! And words! One day, I learned about the meaning of the word *scimitar* up close when I came home from grade school. I was minding my own business getting dinner ready and trying to figure out how to cook a pound of sausage (I thought I had it; I peeled all the skin off) when I heard crazy, swooping sounds coming from the third floor.

When I got up there, I found #1 Italian Son and the Midigan stabbing the walls in the back bedroom with a scimitar they had bought at Paulie the Junkman's. Thank God they found the scimitar first, because if the Italian Madman found it first, he would probably kill the Woman Who Ordered the Peep Assassination or one of us with it. They kept stabbing and stabbing the wall and would not stop. I went into my role; I was Richard Widmark in *Time Limit*. I had to figure this all out before the adults came home. There was more to this story than met the eye.

So I pulled the Midigan out of the room, and in his struggle, he tripped and fell down the stairs. #1 Italian Son was still laughing while I ran down to check on the casualty at the bottom of the stairs. The Midigan was bleeding from his mouth; two of his teeth were broken. He got up and ran away. The moral of this story was that unless #1 Favorite Son told the truth, the whole truth, and nothing but the truth, I was getting blamed. In the long run, #1 Italian Son got off easy, the Midigan lost a few teeth, and I got to clean up all the blood and got blamed for not keeping a lid on things. I also learned it is not a good idea to remove the skin on the sausage before you fry it.

The Woman Who Ordered the Peep Assassination was playing her favorite record, "Kansas City" (she went out and bought a new one), over and over again. She was at her kitchen post making gravy. #1 Italian Son and the Midigan were running the streets, and the Italian Madman was sitting in his favorite chair with one leg over

the arm and a copy of the *Bulletin* covering the top half of his body
while he was calling out orders to me:

"Look up *bourgeois*."

"Look up *cross-pollination*."

When I had a few minutes and could sneak outside for a while,
Favorite Cousin made me a permanent ender. I had to be useful;
either you could jump double Dutch or you couldn't. At least I had
escaped the house for a little while.

When things got slow or a little crazy on our street, I could
walk up the street to my grandmother's house or down the alley to
my other grandmother's house. I had plenty of relatives everywhere.
One of my mother's sisters lived down the street, and one lived up
the street. Two of my father's sisters lived up the street. It got a little
rough, all this family around, especially when you did something
wrong. We had an Italian grapevine long before Gladys Knight and
the Pips first released the song.

The Woman Who Ordered the Peep Assassination was good
with one-liners.

"There is nothing wrong with you. It's only in your head." This
one I found particularly hard to figure out. Your brain is in your
head, and it is in charge of your body. If something is only in your
head, wouldn't that mean that it could be pretty much everywhere?

"You're a big fancy-pants in school, aren't you? I'll teach you to
be a big fancy-pants."

"You are not the boss of me. I am the boss of you. Remember
that."

Somehow I knew I could never forget.

Soon after, the woman chose another husband who had a quiet strength about him. He didn't verbally abuse her, but then he hardly spoke or paid any attention to her at all.

"At least," the woman's battered mother told her repeatedly, "he doesn't beat you."

The woman felt so lonely.

8

Peppercorn

The Women Who Ordered the Peep Assassination introduced me as "my daughter, who never learned how to make homemade macaroni" whenever we met someone new. On Sunday mornings when the Italian Madman was acting nuts or Favorite Cousin was learning how to make homemade macaroni with her, I disappeared around the corner to the convent. The nuns always took me in. The nuns were mostly good to me. I went to the store for them, cleaned the convent (servile work on Sunday, Sister? Mortal sin? Venial sin? Not sure), and they even gave me a piano lesson or two.

The first time I saw a box of Kotex in their bathroom closet, I almost fainted. I could not confess this one in confession; I felt like a real chicken. Who would have thought that nuns got their period? Not me. What if Father didn't know that nuns got their period, either? I didn't want to be the one to break it to him. I was still dealing with the Woman Who Ordered the Peep Assassination's joyous papal proclamation that "Your daughter is a woman now" to the Italian Madman as he stuffed his face with early dinner this particular Sunday afternoon.

Sometimes I called the Woman Who Ordered the Peep Assassination *the Italian Opera Star* in my mind. We had gotten the pool privilege; we finally belonged to the pool. I came home from swimming, made sure no one was in the bathroom, and went in to take my bathing suit off.

Then I got a big, red surprise.

I had prepared ahead of time and written a letter to the Kotex company. The pad, belt, and booklet arrived in a plain, brown envelope. Any stupido knew a plain, brown envelope was the first tip-off. Grandmom down the Alley used to say in Italian that I was born with a pencil in my hand; I was always writing. I was just like an adult, only I was a kid.

The Woman Who Ordered the Peep Assassination pushed me from the bathroom, down the stairs, and into the kitchen. The Italian Madman was raining large amounts of chicken soup with bay leaves onto his dish and drowning mountain-sized chunks of Italian bread in the broth. He didn't look up. He said nothing.

I wanted to go under that space at the bottom of the kitchen sink where the crab went after it climbed out of the pot it was cooking in and fell onto the floor (more on this later).

The men would get up when it was still dark and go crabbing. They said women were not allowed, because there was nowhere for us to pee. They said they peed off the side of the boat. The way I figured it, that was a lame excuse. We didn't care; we were glad to be rid of all of them. Life was kinder when the men were not around.

I tried to get the poor crab out from under the sink; I knew he could hear his buddies shrieking in the pot on the stove and scraping the underside of the lid with their claws. This guy under the sink did not want to be cooked. He did not want Italian ladies using their crochet hooks to pick out all the meat from his body to eat it after he was cooked. I did not reach under the sink, because I was afraid of him pinching me with his claws. I knew his fear won when I could smell something bad in the kitchen a day later, and I knew the smell was coming from under the sink.

I wished I could be a crab and my home was in the ocean far away. But then the Italian Madman might catch me and bring me back. One time, we went on a rare family trip to Atlantic City. He walked out really far into the ocean and took me with him. I was afraid if we got too far away that he would drown me and nobody would know. I would disappear in the ocean water and never be seen again. I would never reach my sixteenth birthday. He tried to keep me close as the water got deeper and did not get it when I kept moving away from him.

I was more afraid of him than the whole Atlantic Ocean. I had safety-pinned a piece of dry garlic in the bra of my bathing suit for good measure before we left the house, just in case he wanted to be nice for a change. If it worked to scare Dracula, it just might work for him. What was I thinking? He ate a ton of garlic every night—no luck here.

My math book said a ton equals two thousand pounds. This is a United States short ton. The English ton is called a long ton, and it equals 2,240 pounds. No time to figure out the long- and short-ton thing in the middle of the Atlantic Ocean when I was on the verge of being drowned. I would make a note to look it up later if I survived. Just in case, I also pinned a tiny miraculous medal to the inside of my bathing suit too.

There was a time when the Woman Who Ordered the Peep Assassination was on a kick for me and him to be close. It was obvious he did not like me, and I knew for certain that I did not like him. When he was taking his after-dinner nap, she made me lie in bed with him. He must have thought I was her, because when he rolled over one time, he put his huge, short Italian leg on top of me.

An episode of *Ramar of the Jungle* was saturating my brain. Somehow a woman got shut out of her jungle hut and was screaming to be let in, but there was nobody to let her in. All of a sudden, a whole sea of blood started to flow under the closed door from the side where the woman was locked out. In the background, I could hear a panther growling.

I thought I was going to do something I had not done in a long time. I did not want to pee a waterfall all over the bed. I prayed to Saint Jude, the patron saint of hopeless cases (I thought this qualified), to get me out of this jam really quickly. There seemed to be no way out. It occurred to me that now that I was a woman, I needed to somehow handle these things. I would pretend I was a water dog, very comfortable in water, and I would go from there.

A miracle! He rolled the other way, and I was free. Then I escaped. Thank God! If peeing on somebody made you have a baby with them, I did not want to have a baby with the Italian Madman. I already had several crazy kids to look after in this family, plus Favorite Cousin. That was enough.

Every Sunday, the boy member of the only set of twins in my grade school fainted before Holy Communion. I wondered if that was a sin; I wonder if it was mortal or venial. I had to figure it out, so I filled wrote down the four qualities of a mortal sin and filled them in:

> Problem: fainting in church before Holy Communion
> Grievous matter? Yep. Pretty bad.
> In front of everybody in church? Really bad.
> Sufficient reflection? Yep. He had to be thinking about
>   doing it. He did it every Sunday.
> Full Consent of the Will? Probably not; he looked like
>   he did not know what hit him when he went down.

I figured there was no mortal sin for him there. The poor guy, like the rest of us, had fasted for twenty-four hours so that he could receive the Body of Christ. This knocked out eating and drinking most of your Saturday so that you could receive Communion on Sunday. Somehow, this guy needed food more than the rest of us did. He needed something to drink. He wanted water, he wanted Tang orange drink, and he could not have it. If Tang was good enough for John Glenn, it should be good enough for anybody, but not if you were fasting for Communion.

So he always fainted. So they put something (peppercorns?) under his nose, scooped him up, and carried him out as the rest of us kept saying our Latin prayers from our missals and singing our Latin hymns with the nun clicking her clicker to remind us to kneel. This guy probably did not even get a chance to say the Centurion's prayer before he passed out.

O Lord, I am not worthy, but only say the word. And I shall be healed.

I know he didn't get a chance to say it, because if he did, Jesus would have healed him on the spot. Hungry, thirsty, fasted, unhealed, fainted, and carried out. No Body of Christ today for you, palsy-walsy. He could always peel the top layer of the Torrone candy off at home and pretend it was Holy Communion. I never saw him take Communion one time in church.

On the girls' side of church, his twin sister looked like she wanted to die. Who would not help a brother passing out in front of everybody? Especially a twin? Maybe she was nervous and it did not feel real. I can remember wanting to murder #1 Italian Son in cold blood a few times, but that was when he did something nuts. Faint guy was innocent here. He was one of the eight million stories in the Naked City too. She'd better confess this one. The Good Samaritan helped a person he didn't even know, Sister said. This was your friggin' brother.

A big concern of my classmates and mine was the pagan babies. We did not know where they lived or what they looked like, but Sister always brought them up, especially during Lent when we were Lenting on some favorite food or trying to fix a bad habit. We saved our pennies in our mite boxes. Come to think of it, *mite* is a homonym of *might*. No mighting when it came to money in the mite boxes. Sister expected us to fill our mite boxes to the top. We were good little Catholic boys and girls.

Sister told us in class to write about a color. How does one write about a color? I thought there might be more interesting things to say if I wrote about a color that I didn't like. It turns out I don't like any colors—only black, just like the colors on the Rorschach blots. So I wrote each color on a small piece of paper and put all the little papers in the Woman Who Ordered the Peep Assassination's gravy pot. Then I pulled out green … I asked Sister for tips, and she said I could not write about grass being green or peas being green.

The Color Green

I hate the color green. What is the purpose of the color green? I never wear green. When I eat onion, I feel green. Sometimes peppercorns look green. Celery and parsley are green. The tips of carrots are green. Green is the color of the grasshoppers that Favorite Cousin and I experiment on down the basement. We catch them (not easy to do; they are great leapers), we decapitate them with the Woman Who Ordered the Peep Assassination's kitchen scissors, and then we investigate the long, stringy, tobacco-like substance that they used to spit out under our magnifying glass that we pretend is a microscope.

Grasshoppers are interesting insects. We watch them chew their food; I found a double-decker grasshopper once—green on green. I found in the *Encyclopedia Britannica* that girl grasshoppers are bigger than boy grasshoppers.

I saw a movie once called *Beginning of the End*. In this movie, giant grasshoppers attack a city. They eat all the crops and then start eating the people. The grasshoppers were as big as our school bus that picks up all the kids that ride the bus. The scientists in the movie trick the giant grasshoppers with recorded mating calls into Lake Michigan, and all the giant grasshoppers drown.

I think of nature when I think of the color green. Some of the Japanese beetles we catch have green heads. We tie one of their thorny legs up with string and then spin them in circles over our heads. We feel bad when the beetle flies off the string and just the leg stays attached to the string. We figure if Chester in *Gunsmoke* could make it work with a bum leg, the beetle would figure it out with a missing leg. We always know when beetles are around by inspecting leaves. When we find leaves eaten all between the lines on them and just the lines left, we knew that beetles had feasted.

The other day, my father came home with chocolate-covered grasshoppers and ants and wanted me to eat them. Kids in the neighborhood take all the green lights off the lightning bugs and make a light-up ring that glows in the dark. The way I figure it, it takes around nine lightning-bug lights to make one lightning-bug ring. I can't do this; it feels cold-blooded.

Frogs are green, and some snakes are green. Dragons are green. On Saint Patrick's Day, all the Irish people in the Irish church celebrate Saint Patrick by wearing the color green. One of the colors of the Irish flag is green. Leprechauns are green. One of the traffic lights is the color green. It means *go*. "Where do I go from here?" Bananas that are not ripe yet are green. Salad is green. Algae is green; money is green. Yellow and blue mixed together make green. The painter Vincent van Gogh used the color viridian, which looks green. The Green Knight is found in the legend of King Arthur. Paper money is sometimes called a "greenback" because the back of the one-dollar bill is green.

The priest vestments are sometimes green; Sister says it is the color of hope. I heard a saying once— "Green with envy"—so maybe green is the color of envy too. Mona Lisa is wearing green; army camouflage clothes are green. My mother's birthstone ring is green. My grandparents had green cards when they came to America.

The End

In a desperate attempt to fill her heart with love and her life with meaning and hope, the woman had baby after baby. Four babies in a row. She almost died with her fourth baby, and the doctor told her that another baby would kill her. Her children kept her busy and filled up her life. She read to them and taught them how to read. Her quiet, strong husband began to distance himself more and more from her.

She felt so tired.

9

Salt

This time was different. I felt like the salt after the priest blessed the house. We never used it; we just threw it away after we gave the priest a five-spot and he left. She had thrown me away like the salt.

The Woman Who Ordered the Peep Assassination left the house and did not take any of us with her. I had a feeling she was up to no good when I saw her putting things in a suitcase I had bought at Paulie the Junkman's for a quarter.

Favorite Cousin taught me how to play this game on the sidewalk. It was a series of jumps on sidewalk cracks and lines.

Step on a crack, break your mother's back
Step on a line, break your mother's spine.

I played the game once but could not say the words. I wouldn't wish those things on my worst enemy, let alone the Woman Who Ordered the Peep Assassination.

She moved into an apartment downtown on Chestnut Street. I met her one day (and took Philadelphia Transit Company both ways), and she bought me a fancy dress. I was going to the boys' high school prom.

I remember one time when I went to the boys' high school football game and the colored guys were singing a song:

Saint Tommy Mambo ole, ole
Saint Tommy Mambo ope e do
It's in my ear (oh yeah), I cannot hear
It's in my mouth (oh yeah), I cannot talk
It's in my eyes (oh yeah), I cannot see
It's in my legs (oh yeah), I cannot walk
Saint Tommy Mambo ole, ole
Saint Tommy Mambo ope e do

I was singing this song in my head when all of a sudden she was walking by the front of the house with nonchalance (synonym—unconcerned, indifferent) on a Sunday morning. The Italian Madman and I were sitting out front on chairs doing our look-up-the-word thing. I had Paulie the Junkman's dictionary on my lap.

We looked like a family scene from an episode of *The Munsters*. Eddie had written an essay for school called "My Parents: An Average American Family." They were anything but average.

The only problem was the essay was written in blood.

We were anything but average. No access to blood, as no one was bleeding lately. When I saw her passing by, I wanted to pull her back in the house. At the same time, I wanted her to escape far away. One of us had to. I wanted to holler at her (confess this really soon: Fourth Commandment "Honor Thy Father and Thy Mother"). She had left me alone with all these *faccia bruttes*.

The funny thing was that the Italian Madman was nicer when she was not around. This was one for the books that #1 Italian Son and I always tried to figure out. So she passed by me and the Italian Madman sitting out front with her head high, not looking at us.

And what did the Italian Madman do? He shouted after her, "Keep going! We don't need you, anyway! *She* has gravy on the stove already!"

Sure, I admit I never stuck around to learn how to make homemades, but I knew how to make a good gravy; I had watched her and Grandmom up the Street cook gravy every Sunday of my whole life.

My homemade gravy was a cross between the Woman Who Ordered the Peep Assassination's gravy and Grandmom up the Street's gravy. I added things to my gravy that the Woman Who Ordered the Peep Assassination never would and that maybe Grandmom up the Street would. I threw in chicken legs, minced garlic, bay leaves, a whole onion, a few celery stalks (only for flavor, and they were removed later), whole carrots (the same), cut-up parsley, whole peppercorns, and a generous amount of salt.

Looking up the word *cross* in the dictionary got me thinking about Jesus's cross. The only one we ever learned in grade school was the plain up-and-down Latin cross. The encyclopedia had many different styles of crosses.

I found all the styles of crosses interesting and decided to draw them for when I pretend-taught out front. Then I could show all the kids that came to my "school" that there were different ways of looking at the same kind of thing sometimes. I was going to memorize them and know them for the future. Sister says no learning is ever wasted. I have to look up those little apostrophe-type marks over a few names of the crosses; I wonder what they mean.

The types of crosses are:

Latin (my favorite, got this one)
Calvary
Patriarchal
Papal
Lorraine
Greek
Celtic
Maltese
Saint Andrew's
Tau
Pommée
Botonée

Fleury
Avellan
Moline
Formée
Fourchée
Crosslet
Quadrate
Potent

A happy feeling had come over me as I looked at all these crosses in my pretend-teach book. *A finito!* (Finished!) as Grandmom up the Street would say when she was done cooking her gravy (and probably my duck).

Only now, my goose was cooked.

Why did the Italian Madman have to make that comment about my gravy to the Woman Who Ordered the Peep Assassination? For sure, I would never live this one down. Who did I think I was making gravy when she was staying away from him purposely and trying to pay him back?

The Woman Who Ordered the Peep Assassination came home in time for the prom. I was getting dressed. Like clockwork (like sands through the hourglass, so are the days of our lives), they were fighting again. I called my date, and his mother told me to take my clothes around to their house and get dressed there. After that, when I play the Woman Who Ordered the Peep Assassination's 45 rpm record of "Earth Angel," I think of my date's mother.

As things went in the house, I was beaten the least. I try to figure this out again and again, but I cannot. I was grateful, with a broken record playing in my head. Just like all the 45s I had to pick up after they had broken them all on the last dance night, I am broken too.

The nun in high school wanted us to write a poem about a figure who impressed us in some way. I wrote a poem about a Negro man I used to see all the time on Fifty-Second Street.

The Soda Can Man

Have you seen him?
He walks that crazy walk
And talks that crazy talk,
Pepsi, Coke, ginger ale—
They are all there.
The shopping cart he pushes
Full of them—all empty.
Too tall, too thin,
Unkempt
He shuffles.
A kid would not be caught dead
In his sneakers.
The pants—way too long,
Way too baggy.
The jacket—to die for.
Did a dying man wear it
Before him?
An old face
Strangely handsome,
Worn,
Bearded.
A hat sideways,
Baseball cap—old like him,
Worn like him.
Who loves you as
You walk your crazy walk
And talk that crazy talk?

One day, the Woman Who Ordered the Peep Assassination overheard one of the neighborhood ladies talking in the pizza parlor, and she was saying that a Midigan woman met the Italian Madman on the job every day and brought him lunch. They sat and talked together while he ate the lunch she brought him.

What, the Woman Who Ordered the Peep Assassination

wondered, did he do with the good Italian lunch meat and pepper-and-egg sandwiches she made him every day? What did this *puttana* think she was doing having lunch with another woman's husband? The Italian Madman never had conversations with her over food.

At the time, the Italian Madman's car was mysteriously missing in action, because he discovered that a stolen car could be traced by a number on the engine. So he borrowed Favorite Uncle's car to go to visit the girlfriend in her second-floor apartment. Favorite Uncle's jacket was hanging on the hook in the backseat when the gig went down (remember this for later; it is Sherlock Holmes stuff).

The Woman Who Ordered the Peep Assassination enlisted Favorite Cousin on the Italian Madman's side of the family to take her to the Midigan woman's apartment. She went to the second-floor apartment and banged on the door. When no one answered, she broke the bricks made of glass on the side of the door (she had brought a hammer in her pocketbook, just in case she needed it). Then she reached in and unlocked the door.

The way she tells it, she got in the apartment just in time to see the Italian Madman jumping out the second-story window. She pushed past the Midigan *puttana* (she was not the main issue here) and looked out the window just in time to see the Italian Madman speeding up the street in Favorite Uncle's car.

It was Sunday. I was home watching the gravy. No one was home when I came home from Mass, and I did not want it to burn. The Italian Madman came into the house and assumed his place on the chair with his leg over the arm. He looked a little out of breath. He picked up the *Bulletin* (we were already done looking up words earlier; I had looked up *hydrocortisone* and *balsam*). So what was he doing now? And he was acting all nonchalant. I must have looked at him crazy, because he bellowed into the kitchen, "Take a picture! It'll last longer!"

So I figured we would be doing a rerun of that morning's words, or maybe he had more words that he needed me to look up.

Then the Woman Who Ordered the Peep Assassination came busting through the front door.

"I saw you, you son of a b——"

At the time, I am sure she was not aware that she was cursing Grandmom up the Street (why would she curse her? Grandmom up the Street had taught her how to make homemades). I made a note in my head to teach this to the kids in the neighborhood when we played school; when you say "son of a b——," you are not reaching your intended target but your intended target's mother.

"You are not getting away with this."

"What are you talking about? I am here reading the paper. What is your problem?"

"Don't try to buffalo me. I saw the jacket in the car [key piece of evidence here]. I know you were in that apartment. You jumped out the window."

All of a sudden, I remembered what happened to me the night before. I woke up in the middle of the night, and I saw a figure standing by my bed. It had on long robes and two funny pointy things sticking out on either side of the top of his (her?) head. It was holding something in its right hand, like the staff that turned to serpents that I saw Moses holding at the movies.

Then it dawned on me.

It was Desiree! She was coming around because a little birdie had told her that I would be scared soon. I started praying then in the middle of the night and continued my prayers at Mass the next morning for the special intention (whatever it was, I just knew it was coming soon).

"You're nuts. Ask la strega. I have been here for the past hour or two reading the paper. What the hell is wrong with you?"

So at the same time I was listening to them scream at each other and praying to God and asking Desiree to come there, I was saying in my mind, *Don't ask me ... please don't ask me ... I do not want to lie ... it is Sunday here ... I just went to confession yesterday ...*

"Don't act innocent. I don't have to ask her. I saw you. You are a f—— liar."

So nonchalantly (remember this meaning from before), he stood up and went up the stairs to the second floor.

"What's the matter? Cat got your tongue?" she said to the back of his head as she follows him up.

Here we go again, I thought as I followed her up.

We were in single file, the three of us, like three different parts of an ant's body, separate yet attached. He was the head, she was the upper body, and I was the lower body part. I thought, *This life-debt thing is really beginning to get on my nerves.*

At the top of the stairs, she immediately went into her Italian opera star routine. She knelt down on the floor, her eyes up to heaven, her arms crossed over her chest. I was becoming a regular picture study expert; she looked like the picture Mary Magdalene by the artist Ary Scheffer I saw in the encyclopedia.

"Dear God, if he is lying, give me a sign," she prayed out loud.

I really quickly analyzed the type of prayer this was. Prayer could be praise prayer, intercessory prayer, or thanksgiving prayer. She wasn't praising anybody or anything, and it was not around Thanksgiving time. I went with intercessory prayer (synonym—ask, request). She was asking God to intercede, and she wanted a sign.

The nuns in school always said to be careful of what you ask God for, and I was pretty careful with that, because Jesus is always listening even when you don't want Him to. The Woman Who Ordered the Peep Assassination was either not thinking or she didn't care.

She just wanted her sign.

Immediately, the Italian Madman grabbed his chest, and his body slammed into the wall. He was trying to hold himself up. I was looking at the hallway clock, getting ready to wait an hour after he hit the floor and then call the police.

The Woman Who Ordered the Peep Assassination screamed

at me to call the police right away and to tell them to bring an ambulance. Was she losing her mind? This could be our big break.

I wanted to do my best Jimmy Cagney impersonation from *Angels with Dirty Faces* right then:

> *Shut up! Now, look, you don't know anything about this, see?*
> *Oh, come on, don't be such an angel. You wanna get the center built, don't you? Well, go ahead—get it started.*

I ran to the bathroom to get him a glass of water (we used paper Dixie cups) and then ran and got the blanket off his bed to make him comfortable. Then I ran downstairs to get the olive oil. I couldn't believe how all Sister's instructions were coming in handy lately, because I was going to give him Extreme Unction next.

I had looked it up. I thought it would be a great idea if I ever needed it. He never went to confession. Extreme Unction was good for when you were dying *and* if you needed your sins forgiven. Paulie the Junkman's dictionary said, *unction* was "the act of anointing as a rite of consecration or healing." I did not have time to get the olive oil blessed; we would make do with what we had on the stove.

All I had to do, the dictionary said, was to anoint his eyes, ears, nose, lips, hands, and loins, if possible. I looked up *loins* too. It was the area near you know what (the fig leaf part). No way was I anointing *that*. This was my father here. Are you kidding me? The shorter version of Extreme Unction was just anointing the forehead with oil. I would go with that one and say, "Through this holy unction, may the Lord pardon thee whatever sins or faults thou hast committed."

It would feel kind of funny saying "thee" and "hast," but directions were directions. I had an honor code like the soldiers in those military movies; I could never leave a man on the battlefield.

When he came home from the hospital, he looked different. He was moving more slowly—kind of like the way my Thunder moved after he strangled him. Thunder even went up to him when he came through the front door and tried to lick his hand. He kicked Thunder away with his dusty, pointy, black Italian-bar-around-the-corner shoe.

He could not go back to work. Great, now he was home all the time. He was quieter (but still cursed a blue streak) and did not keep the Woman Who Ordered the Peep Assassination up all night arguing every single night. She was mad at him all the time now. She moved him out of their bedroom and set up two single beds in the back bedroom—one bed for him and one for #1 Italian Son. #1 Italian Son's bed was under the bullet hole in the ceiling. Very cozy.

Was she nuts?

In my eyes, the Italian Madman could not be trusted, especially in a closed room, with a contender that he had defeated in the past and who now could very possibly defeat him.

I was half-asleep, but I could hear #1 Italian Son creeping up the stairs. Dear God, it was after midnight, and his curfew was 11:00 p.m. I fell asleep then and dreamed the bride dream for the fifty millionth time. I was a beautiful bride walking up the aisle of my parish church in a beautiful white gown with a long train. My hands were folded in front of me. The only problem was that when I got to the altar, everybody in the church was looking for the groom, and he was nowhere to be found. As signs went, this did not look like a good one for me.

I was forced awake by a large thud sound and a muffled scream. I knew it had to be the thud maker at it again. Even though the Italian Madman seemed weaker now, he was still mean and still strong. The tide did seem to be turning slowly in our favor lately, but not fast enough.

He had waited until #1 Italian Son fell asleep after he crept up the stairs and came in late. Then he got #1 Italian Son's heavy work boots (both of them) and slammed his handsome, sleeping face with them. That was where the scream came from.

I stayed in my room and cried sad tears, crazy tears, revengeful tears. I pretended in my mind that I was doing water ballet. I was Esther Williams in the rerun of *The Million Dollar Mermaid*. Somehow, it always comes back to me and the water. I do not want to be waterproof. I imagine that water soothes me and washes away all my sins and all my fears. When the Italian Madman went downstairs for a cigarette, I sneaked a hot water bottle into #1 Italian Son to put on his face. For some reason, right then, I started thinking about my Betsy Wetsy doll.

I remembered when #1 Italian Son threw my Betsy Wetsy doll down the stairs. Her head broke, and her eyes stayed back in her head. I thanked God I had not just fed her, or for sure she would have peed her panties.

The Italian Madman had pulled a real sneak job on #1 Italian Son. The Woman Who Ordered the Peep Assassination would always say that the Italian Madman was pulling a gaslight on her. I looked the movie *Gaslight* up. Was he trying on purpose to make her crazy and using #1 Italian Son to cinch the deal?

I made up a prayer and asked Jesus to save #1 Italian Son.

"Please, Jesus, don't let his head be broken like my Betsy Wetsy doll. Please, Jesus, save him like Daniel in the lion's den. Keep King Darius [the Italian Madman] away from him, and please let the Italian Madman repent of doing mean things to #1 Italian Son like King Darius did for Daniel. I promise, Jesus, to pray three times a day, like Daniel did. You are my God! Jesus, please make me waterworn. Provide a waterway for our escape."

I wanted to murder the Italian Madman a lot like they did that nice man in the movie *In Cold Blood*. If I confessed it, I knew Father could not blab since he had made an oath not to tell people's sins. I would have to be careful of blood on the sole of my flip-flop. That's the way the killer was caught in the movie; they traced him to a cat's paw emblem on his shoes, which had left an imprint on the floor in the Clutter home. If I needed the shoes repaired that I wore during the murder and brought them to Nunzy, the shoemaker around the corner, he was one of them and would turn me in on a dime.

The children grew up quickly, and the woman, seeking a meaning in her life, entered nursing school. When the woman's quiet, strong husband became an alcoholic and left her, the abandoned little girl resurrected herself in the woman's mind and heart.

The woman and the little girl resurrected inside her felt bereft.

10

Bouillon

Meanwhile, the Woman Who Ordered the Peep Assassination had taken a job as a cook at the Italian club around the corner (yep, the same place where the Italian Madman went every night and wore his pointy, black Italian-bar-around-the-corner shoe). And best of all, she wanted me to be a waitress for her. I figured this might add a little excitement to my life and get me out of the house a little bit. I might even get to see the Italian Madman in action and try to figure him out.

At the Italian club around the corner, we made meatballs, homemade macaroni, ravioli, and cavatelli. Then I got to hear fifty million more times every Sunday when we were there cooking how I never learned to make homemades.

For the first time in my life, I figured out that *we* are who we are, and *they* are who they are. The only people that came into the club to eat are Italian, part-Italian, married to Italian, or Italian wannabes. Everyone had to pass inspection at the door.

I found it odd that my favorite colored people from Grandmom down the Alley's street usually did not come to sit down and eat at the Italian club around the corner. I thought about the song "The In Crowd." Anyone who got into the Italian club was a member of the in crowd just because they were who they were (something Italian).

I even began to understand the picture called *The Gleaners* better. In the case of *The Gleaners*, I found I was on the side of the middle-class people who were already accepted in society and not on the side of the peasants who were picking wheat in the picture. Another way of looking at it is that I was a gleaner too—a gleaner of ideas, a gleaner of words, a gleaner of the water level in tricky waters.

The people from Grandmom down the Alley's street often come in for takeout, though.

"I would like an order of them *dungaree crab* legs."

"I am sorry, sir; we do not have crab legs."

"Miss, I would like a six-pack of Milleress Lifess."

"I am sorry, sir; we only have Miller Light beer. Is that what you mean?"

"Be sure to include tobacco sauce with that fish."

"I am sorry, sir; we only have fish on Festa Dei Sette Pesci [Feast of the Seven Fishes] around Christmastime. Do you mean Tabasco sauce?"

"Miss, I would like an order of chicken parmagon."

"Yes, sir. Coming right up." (I could figure that one out.)

"Miss, do you serve horse ovaries?"

"I am sorry, sir. Do you mean hors d'oeuvres?"

"I still remembers your aunts shooting up Stiles Street. They is my heroes."

"Oh, okay."

"I remember your grandmama. She had that twisted-up back thing goin' on. She gives me Easter bread one time that your other grandmother had made. It was hard as a rock. When I told her I did not want her hard, old bread, she said, 'Mah, whatsa matta fah you, you craz? The Italian Easter bread, she is a supposa be hard. You justa dunka ina you coffee. *Delizioso!*' And you know what, girlie? She was 100 percent right. I misses your grandmama. She was one of us. It wasn't even one of us that stoles her TV. It was somebody that was a friend of somebody on the street. Your aunts was like Annie Oakley reincarnated."

Meanwhile, #1 Italian Son had been stabbed again. The first time, a year earlier, he was stabbed in the back. When I cleaned the wound with water from the sink and changed the bandage, I stretched open the wound between my two hands, as it was not healed yet. I saw something brown. I swear it was his liver.

The second time, he and his best friend were walking home from a double date at the movies when four guys jumped them. This time, they stabbed him in the neck. The doctor at the hospital said the stabbers had just missed #1 Italian Son's jugular vein. I was not allowed to change this wound.

His best friend told me right after #1 Italian Son was stabbed, he grabbed the guy who stabbed him by the back of his head and must have slammed his face down on the sidewalk twenty-five times before the cops came. The other three guys ran away.

When the cops finally came (they were arriving on the scene slower these days), #1 Italian Son had already run into my Aunt up the Street's house, the Woman Who Ordered the Peep Assassination's sister. She was so upset that she kept looking at him and pushing his face into her chest. She had his blood all over her.

"Jesus, please don't let him die," she kept saying over and over.

"Aunt Mary," he rasped to her. "You gotta let me go."

"I am sorry! Am I hurting you more? Are you dying? Please don't die. Your mother will kill me."

"The only way I am going to die," he said, "is if you keep suffocating me with your big breasts."

One day, we had a special takeout order (we served people in the bar and had takeout) for *zuppa maritata* for fifty. Someone in the neighborhood was getting married, and they wanted to serve Italian wedding soup at their house luncheon for the wedding party. I thought I might as well learn how to make it for someone else. The dream I kept having of me as a bride with no groom kind of cemented in my head that I would never have a husband or be able to keep one.

This guy who looked like Barnabas Collins started talking to me a lot when I was working with my mother at the Italian club. All the neighborhood guys told me to stay away from him. The Italian Madman made a comment that I would regret getting involved with him if I ever did. He was almost ten years older than I was. I felt bad for the guy; he seemed weird for some reason. I liked the attention he gave me.

The name *Italian wedding soup* does not come from the wedding-of-two-people idea but from the wedding of ingredients. No wedding for me, palsy-walsy. The only close association happening around me lately was my close association with books and the written word.

My cousin's recipe for Italian wedding soup was easy to follow.

Wedding Soup (Zuppa Maritata)

For Stock:

5–6 large chicken breasts, with skin on
4 garlic cloves, halved
3 dried bay leaves
2 large onions, quartered
6 large celery stalks, halved with the leaves
6 carrots, peeled and halved
6 sprigs, flat-leaf Italian parsley
10 peppercorns
Salt to taste
2 cubes chicken bouillon
2 1/2 gallons cold water

For Soup:

1 cup pastina
1 pound frozen crinkle-cut carrots, thawed
2 pounds frozen chopped spinach, thawed and drained
8 extra-large eggs
1 cup Romano cheese

For Meatballs:

1 pound lean ground beef
1 teaspoon dried parsley
1 teaspoon dried basil
Salt and pepper to taste
2 extra-large eggs
1/2 cup dried unseasoned bread crumbs
1/2 cup oil for frying

Sister asked us to write an essay about something we were familiar with in our lives, and she gave us this highfalutin quotation she wanted us to use in it:

Nostalgia for what we have lost is more bearable than nostalgia for what we have never had.

(*The Neurotic Notebook*, 1960)

After I read the quote many times, I began to think about its meaning and about what did have meaning in my life. For some reason, I kept thinking about water. Somewhere down the line, much later when I am older, I will make peace with the world for the childhood that I can never find and especially for the childhood I could never have. Water has helped me figure some of it out so far.

The Word *Water*

There are many words in the English language that have the word *water* as their base. Therefore, the word *water* can be used in many different ways with many different meanings.

There is something to be said for plain old H_2O (chemical compound for water). It is essential for life. Its chemical name is dihydrogen monoxide, which just means it has two parts hydrogen and one part oxygen. I have come a long way in my life since I first learned the formula for water. One of the books I am reading now says that water is a life-giver. Salt and sugar dissolve easily in water. Water freezes at 0° centigrade and boils at 100° centigrade.

Here is an interesting quote:

Nostalgia for what we have lost is more bearable than nostalgia for what we have never had.

When I first read this quote, it did not look like it could pertain to water. However, as I often think about the influence of water in my life and nostalgia seems to be about life memories, it just might work. I fit the definition of a "scholar of the first water." I try to do my best at schoolwork, and I try to do my best at home. My mother never goes to church or confession, but she loves Psalm 23. One line in the psalm is David saying that Jesus leads him beside the still waters. Maybe my mother wants to be near still water because her life with her family is anything but still. She runs away from us sometimes, but she always comes back. Maybe she wants to be peaceful and rid of all of us, someplace near water.

I was baptized with water when I was in infant. I drink Philadelphia fluoridated water and wash with water every day of my life. I wash off the ashes Father puts on my forehead on Ash Wednesday with water. I drink Grandmother down the Alley's iced tea that she makes with water. I get wet in the fireplug water. I go to Shanahan Pool, and I am weightless and sinless in its water. My younger brother and I went to Memorial Hall once to try out a different swimming pool, and we noticed that everyone in the pool was looking at us funny. We couldn't figure it all out until Charles (one of my neighbors who I had a fight with and who now was my friend) came up to us and told us, "You is the only white folks in this here pool. You Italian folks gots guts."

I looked in the Italian phrasebook at the library for a phrase that has water in it. I could not find one, so I made up my own. It is like an aspiration that contains the word *water*; I am working on memorizing it, because my spirit hydroplanes when I say aspirations.

Jesus, *stare tiene la testa alta de acqua.*

This just means "Jesus, keep my head above water."

My encyclopedia says when a body of water freezes, only the top layer of the water freezes, which helps insulate (prevents the transfer of electricity, heat, and sound) life below. This is a good thing, because life below the top layer is then preserved. My mind and soul (sometimes my kid mind thinks they are the same thing) are safe below the surface; they are preserved and do not drown.

Life is a series of water miracles that define, protect, and shape me. In my short lifetime so far, I have probably used a pool full of water making macaroni for my family and for the people at the Italian club where I work with my mother as her waitress. I went deep-sea fishing on a date once. I threw up the whole time, and the men who were drinking whiskey did not throw up at all. I thought I was throwing up from eating a Tastykake lemon pie (lemon is not my favorite; it is what they had on the boat). Turns out, the captain had missed me when he was giving out Dramamine to all the fishers that day to ward off their seasickness.

When the neighborhood guys sell water chestnuts on the corner every Christmas, I am the first in line. (They do not contain water; I am not sure why they are called *water* chestnuts.)

When the skin around my nails gets green and filled with pus from biting my nails, my mother's mother always makes me soak my hand in the spaghetti bowl filled with water and some salt. My father's mother made duck soup with water and my pet duck.

The old Italian men in my neighborhood talk about a young man who died when he jumped off a high rock at the quarry. The water level was low where he landed, and he hit his head and was killed. Harry the hairdresser, who I work for on Saturdays, says that it is hard to make a water wave in my hair, because my hair is naturally curly.

The watercolors in my life are not lustrous. Sometimes, after my father hurts my mother or my brother, I want to do a good cry, one that would be saturated with water and fill up a watering can. The tears come into my eyes, and then my eyelids act as a dam and hold the tears back. I try every day to achieve a water balance between me and the house I live in.

I looked up the shape of the water once. I have drawn it here to get a good mark on this essay and to remember it for the future.

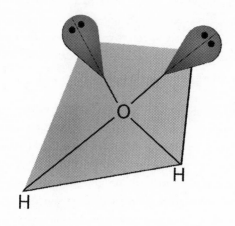

It kind of looks like a kite with no string. It has a hydrogen electron on each side with a lone oxygen electron in the center. Most of the time, I feel alone like the oxygen electron looks in the diagram. I am a vital part of the molecule of my water life. However, I am on the outskirts. Part of an all-alone, high-flying kite molecule with lifesaving water below.

Which gets me to thinking about two other guys who were alone a lot—the Lone Ranger and his sidekick, Tonto. I do not have a buddy for most of my life, but I still try to do good on my own like the Lone Ranger did. I try to save myself, my brother, and my foster brother from them. If I could, I would even save them from them (my mother and father from each other and from themselves), but I am a kid, and I do not know how. I try to fight for what is right like the Lone Ranger. I always try to do my best with what is given to me.

My childhood so far has been continuously waterborne and supported by water. The small kids in the neighborhood shoot each other with water guns. When they let me be the teacher and we do school out front, I tell them about the fear a real gun can bring and the damage a real gun can do.

Circumstances in my young life seem like a water haul, but I am not coming up dry. I am learning every day of my life with water. I am a watermill that houses a waterwheel fed by water, trying to use to my best advantage the sometimes downward direction of the happenings in my life.

The Bible uses water as a blessing. I have been blessed by water in my life. I figure I am laying the foundation for a future life—one that will be above water and not wishy-washy. I alone maintain the water right to me. I never have to use water wings in the water; I am a water strider gliding not so gracefully along the surface of life. I welcome water as a something that can heal me and heal my life. At times, I practice being waterproof and water repellent in order not to drown in the gigantic sea of life.

The End

PS—If you give me a good mark in this essay, Sister, please show it to Sister Daniel when you are at the convent. I know she would be proud; I think this is a really good expository essay on the subject of water.

Stay tuned …

References

Betty Crocker's Good and Easy Cook Book., ed. unknown, 1st ed. New York: Golden Press, 1954.

Bhalla, Jag. *I'm Not Hanging Noodles on Your Ears and Other Intriguing Idioms from Around the World.* Washington, DC: National Geographic, 2009.

DeFabo, Rizzi. *Cooking with Rizzi.* Latrobe, PA: DeFabo Press, 2010.

Klein, Allen. *Winning Words: Quotations to Uplift, Inspire, Motivate and Delight.* New York: Portland House, 2002.

Love, Catherine. *Webster's New World Italian Dictionary.* Boston: Houghton Mifflin Harcourt, 1985.

Mish, Frederick, C., ed. *Webster's Ninth New Collegiate Dictionary.* Springfield, MA: Merriam-Webster, 1983.

Morehead, Philip, D., ed. *Roget's College Thesaurus.* New York: Signet Books, 1985.

The Neurotic Notebook. Accessed 5/21/14. www.quotegarden.com/nostalgia.html

Pickett, Joseph, P., ed. *American Heritage Dictionary.* 4th ed. New York: Random House, 2001.

Ringside by Gus. Accessed 5/21/14. http://www.ringsidebygus.com/boxing-terms.html.

Wikisource. "Departmental Ditties and Ballads and Barrack–Room Ballads/Gunga Din." Accessed 1/17/15. http://en.wikisource.org/wiki/Departmental_Ditties_and_Ballads_and_Barrack_Room_Ball.

Glossary of Words, Abbreviations, and Italian Idioms

Baccala—dried salted codfish

capisco—understand

colored man/guys (term no longer used)—Negro

cooked like a lobster—tired, exhausted

death of the pope—a long time

dungaree crab—Dungeness crab

faccia bruttes—ugly faces

hearts of rabbits—scared

homemades—macaroni made by hand

in the mouth of the wolf—fearful

la strega—witch

mangia—to eat

matta—nutty

Midigan—any non-Italian person

padrone—master

physic—laxative

puttana—whore

sweat seven shirts—work very hard

trident—a three-pronged spear used in Greek mythology, the attribute of a sea god

Instructions for Zuppa Maritata

To Make Stock:

Place all stock ingredients in large pot. Cover and bring to boil. Reduce heat, and simmer 1 to 1 1/2 hours.

To Make Meatballs:

In a large bowl, combine meat, parsley, basil, salt, pepper, eggs, and bread crumbs. Using your hands, mix well, and shape into 1/2-inch balls. Place on oiled sheet pan or plate. When all meatballs have been made, place a large skillet over medium heat. Add oil to skillet, and heat for a few minutes. Working in batches, fry meatballs until brown. Remove from oil with a slotted spoon, and place on paper towel to drain.

To Finish Soup:

Strain broth through a fine-mesh strainer. Let vegetables drain for around 5 minutes to release juices. Set chicken breasts aside to cool. Return broth to stove over medium heat.

Remove chicken from bone, discarding bones and skin. Shred chicken by hand, and return to the broth.

Cook pastina in plenty of salted water until al dente, about 3 minutes. Drain and add pastina to broth. Add carrots and chopped spinach.

In a large bowl, whisk eggs. Bring broth to a steady boil. Gently pour eggs into broth in a steady stream, stirring continuously until all eggs have been added. Add meatballs and Romano cheese. Ladle into bowls and serve.

Soup may be frozen in plastic containers. If freezing, do not add Romano cheese until ready to serve.

Serves: 20

Printed in the United States
By Bookmasters